design & make
precious jewellery
from plastics

St Helens College

LIBRARY

Water Street, St Helens, Merseyside WA10 1PP Tel: 01744 623256

This book is due for return on or before the last date shown below

design & make
precious jewellery from plastics

CHRISTOPHER BOND

BLOOMSBURY
LONDON • NEW DELHI • NEW YORK • SYDNEY

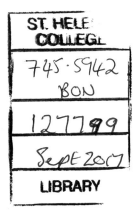
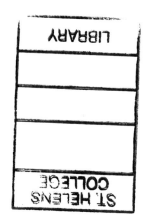
ACKNOWLEDGEMENTS

This book is dedicated to Nicky – thank you for all your support.
And to those who have claimed the fame, remember "it is only by standing on the shoulders of giants"
that you were seen. This book is also dedicated to all the 'giants'.

DISCLAIMER

Everything written in this book is to the best of my knowledge and
every effort has been made to ensure accuracy and safety but neither
author nor publisher can be held responsible for any resulting
injury, damage or loss to either persons or property. Any further
information that will assist in the updating of any future editions
will be gratefully received. Read through all the information in
each chapter before commencing work. Follow all health and safety
guidelines and where necessary obtain health and safety information
from the suppliers. Health and safety information about certain
products can also be found on the Internet.

First published in Great Britain 2013
Bloomsbury Publishing Plc
50 Bedford Square
London WC1B 3DP
www.bloomsbury.com

ISBN: 9781408134450

Copyright © Christopher Bond 2013

All images are copyright of Christopher Bond, unless otherwise
credited, and with the exception of the Art Nouveau Comb on
page 9 which is copyright of the Tadema Gallery, 10 Charlton
Place, Camden Passage, Islington, London N1 8AJ.

A CIP catalogue record for this book is available from the
British Library

Christopher Bond has asserted his rights under the Copyright,
Design and Patents Act 1988 to be identified as the author of
this work.

Commissioning editor: Susan James
Assistant editor: Agnes Upshall
Copy editor: Jane Anson
Cover design: Eleanor Rose
Page layouts: Sydney Soan

This book is produced using paper that is made from wood
grown in managed, sustainable forests. It is natural, renewable
and recyclable. The logging and manufacturing processes
conform to the environmental regulations of the country of
origin.

Printed and bound in China

Contents

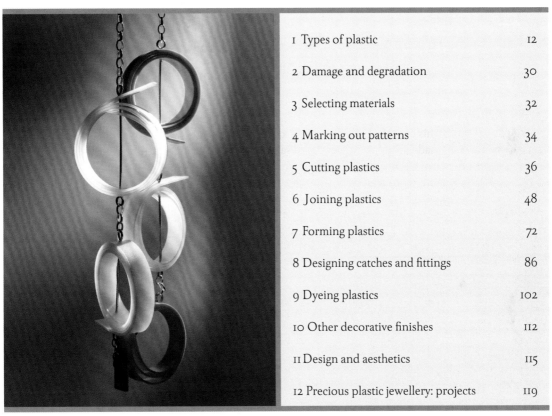

Gill Forsbrook, Chain necklace

about the author

Christopher Bond was educated not as a jeweller but in the sciences. He studied chemistry and physics, and took a degree in life sciences, focusing on molecular genetics. While studying for A-levels, he acquired a keen interest in crafts, beginning with blacksmithing, and developing over nearly 30 years into a passion for working with a wide range of materials and processes, from leather to gold and plastics to textiles.

In 2000 he began working with other jewellers, not as a designer but as a technical jeweller, working to develop techniques and processes that would support the work of others. At this time one of the jewellers brought a sample of sheet polypropylene into the studio, a material that appeared very promising due to its light, colourful and resilient nature. However, initial work proved that the material was very difficult to bond with the adhesives that were available. This may be the reason why polypropylene had failed to make an impact in the contemporary jewellery market.

Determined to solve this problem, Chris began researching the use of polypropylene. It was only when he made the connection between the fact that polypropylene was a thermoplastic and that there were a number of (hot-melt) thermoplastic adhesives on the market, that the first successful bond was achieved and the restraints preventing the use of the plastic began to lift.

Author, Christopher Bond

In the following ten years a significant amount of time and research was invested in solving each of the challenges that the jewellery designs presented, allowing plastics to be used effectively. However, even after ten years there are still few jewellers who work with these materials because, until now, the techniques developed have remained in the studio.

This book explores these techniques in a practical way, providing technical information, principles and suppliers that will allow other jewellers to benefit from the years of research and development and to allow them to explore these exciting materials.

introduction

can plastics ever be described as 'precious'?

As the world's largest producer of polypropylene has a capacity of 7600 kilotonnes per annum, polypropylene will not be valued for its rarity, so why would a jewellery collector be prepared to pay $5000 for a single polypropylene necklace at the Museum of Art and Design in New York?

They were buying it not for its material value but for the quality of its design and the fact that the piece had won a prestigious award for innovation and design. Excellent design has been the subject of many jewellery books, but to realise a design with a material, it is necessary to fully understand the techniques and processes that can be used.

A beautiful piece of jewellery is precious not only for its design but also because of the high quality of production, in every part and every detail.

Some people feel that plastic jewellery can never be precious, though this prejudice may be overcome by combining plastics with traditional materials such as precious metals. The same principle can be seen in some outstanding Art Nouveau jewellery, where semi-precious stones and precious metals have been combined with low-value materials such as horn.

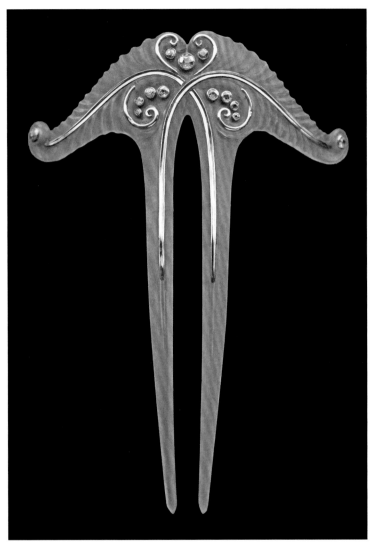

Henri Hamm (1871–1961) Art Nouveau hair comb. Carved blond horn, inlaid with gold and mounted with demantoid garnets. French, c.1900.
Image courtesy of the Tadema Gallery, London.

There is no doubt that these pieces have stood the test of time and are now recognised as works of art in their own right. If jewellery incorporating plastics can be treated in the same way, it is possible that they will be equally valued now and in the future.

working with modern materials

For many years contemporary studio or art jewellery has incorporated the use of a wide range of materials, seeking to produce new and innovative pieces that derive their value from their aesthetic appeal rather than from their material worth. In this field of work the quality of the design and a high standard of finish are prerequisites of truly outstanding work.

Designers of jewellery have been willing to explore and experiment with a wide range of materials and have readily incorporated new material like aluminium (1825), rubber (vulcanised 1830), Bakelite (1909), titanium (1910), and a large number of synthetic plastics, into their work.

With any new material it is necessary to determine how it can be handled, cut, formed, shaped, polished, coloured, secured etc., and this requires a significant amount of research and experimentation. However, with many materials there is now a considerable pool of experience that designers can refer to in order to make this process easier.

Even with this assistance, a designer must understand the nature and properties of a material if they are to be able to produce work that is both aesthetically pleasing and durable enough to wear. Understanding the limitations of the material and the processes used in working with it will allow the designer to push the boundaries of their work and explore their creativity. Therefore, the first task of a designer is to thoroughly acquaint themselves with their chosen material through practical experimentation.

The aim of this book is twofold, first it provides practical, tried and tested techniques for working with modern plastics, particularly acrylic and polypropylene. (Acrylic has been commercially available since 1936, while polypropylene did not appear on the market until 1957.)

Throughout this work consideration will be given to the techniques that can be applied to the materials with a view to producing functional jewellery that has a high standard of finish. Unless otherwise stated, all the techniques described are based on direct experience and are the result of over ten years of practical research and development in an art jewellery studio working as a materials technician.

The secondary function of this work is to provide a model for experimentation that can be applied to any material that a designer may wish to use. A designer may wish to use leather in a design but may not have any experience in working with it. However, by considering what similarities and differences there may be between leather and the materials they already use, they may find they can apply some of the techniques that they have learned to use on leather. For example:

▶ Leather is tough, durable, hard to tear and flexible,
   not unlike polypropylene
▶ Most leather is absorbent, rapidly taking up water,
   very different from polypropylene.

The greater the knowledge of materials and techniques, the more effective this approach becomes and the easier it is for a designer to use new materials effectively.

types of plastic

Since plastics were first developed, there has been a steady increase in the types and sub-types of plastics available. Polymer chemists have developed a range of materials with different properties to suit the varied industrial applications that have been identified. We are surrounded by many objects that have been cast, formed, moulded and fabricated from plastics of one type or another. One extreme example was DuPont's development of Kevlar, a polymer than can be made into fibres and woven into a textile capable of stopping a bullet!

In order to begin to understand the different properties of plastics, it is necessary to provide an overview of the main types available. There are many variations with particular individual properties, so it is advisable to obtain the technical specification for any plastic purchased, to ensure that the designer knows the general properties of the material they are dealing with.

polypropylene (PP)

Polypropylene or polypropene (PP) is a thermoplastic polymer, an addition polymer made from the monomer propylene. It was first polymerised in 1954 and went into full-scale production in 1957. Polypropylene is reasonably economical, and can be made translucent when uncoloured, but it is not as readily made transparent as polystyrene, acrylic or certain other plastics. It is often opaque or coloured using pigments.

DURABILITY

Polypropylene is a strong plastic with good resistance to fatigue. It also exhibits a good resistance to most common chemical solvents, bases and acids. Therefore it is tough and flexible with a good level of durability, giving a springy medium that retains its shape when subjected to knocks and short-term pressure.

HEALTH AND SAFETY

Combustion releases carbon monoxide and carbon dioxide, which represent a hazard to health. For further details you should contact the supplier and request a Material Safety Data Sheet.

COLOURS

Post-polymerisation, and while in a liquid state, polypropylene is blended with pigment. It is then extruded in a wide variety of forms including pellets, fibres, sheets and finished products such as bottles.

It is difficult to produce clear polypropylene and it is most commonly found in opaque or translucent forms. In addition to this some translucent colours are more difficult to produce. This particularly limits the range of reds available in translucent polypropylene.

It has been noted that the clearest, un-pigmented polypropylene sheets have a tendency to be rather brittle compared with translucent and solid colours, which may result in a fracture when scored and folded. Therefore it is recommended that the clearer grades are tested before complex designs are attempted.

The addition of pigments has some impact on the properties of the finished material, and this is most commonly noted in a slight variation in the temperature at which it will soften and melt. So it is advisable to test each colour prior to making up a design.

A typical colour swatch suppled by a manufacturer of polypropylene

SURFACE FINISH

Polypropylene sheets are available in a range of surface finishes. Depending on the production process and manufacturer, the surface finish may even vary from one face to the other. Typical finishes include:

- smooth, e.g. Priplak Cristal
- satin, e.g. Priplak Izilyss
- pearlised, Priplak Opaline
- light texture, e.g. Priplak Opaline
- light ridges, e.g. Priplak Lines
- corrugated texture, e.g. Priplak Coteline
- laminated finish, e.g. Priplak Silkyss
- frosted/metallic with metallic flecks, e.g. Priplak Stardust.

Manufacturers are continually seeking to produce different finishes and effects and frequently produce swatches of samples that show the range of colours, thicknesses and surface finishes. They usually supply samples free of charge, and it is well worth requesting these before beginning the design process.

NB Stockists may not hold stock of all colours and thicknesses, and this can be a limiting factor at times.

RECYCLING AND BIODEGRADABILITY

Polypropylene is commonly recycled, however the main issue that impacts on the level of recycling is the recovery of the items after use. With increasing emphasis on recycling, it is likely that the percentage of polypropylene recovered each year will increase.

Without the addition of UV-absorbing additives and anti-oxidants, polypropylene is susceptible to UV degradation which will result in the breakdown of the polymer and the appearance of surface cracks that become deeper over time as the degradation continues. In jewellery applications it is unlikely that the material will suffer receive sufficient UV exposure to cause any noticeable damage.

Polypropylene is listed under Plastics Recycling Symbol Number 5 – PP.

acrylic (polymethyl methacrylate) (PMMA)

This is a transparent thermoplastic. Chemically, it is the synthetic polymer of methyl methacrylate. It is sold under many trade names, including Policril, Plexiglas, Gavrieli, Vitroflex, Limacryl, R-Cast, Perclax, Perspex, Plazcryl, Acrylex, Acrylite, Acrylplast, Altuglas, Polycast, Oroglass, Optix and Lucite, and is commonly called acrylic glass, simply acrylic, perspex or plexiglas. The material was developed in 1928 in various laboratories and was brought to market in 1933 by the Rohm and Haas Company.

PMMA is often used as a light or shatter-resistant alternative to glass. It is an economical alternative to polycarbonate (PC) when extreme strength is not necessary. It is often preferred because of its moderate properties, easy handling and processing, and low cost, but behaves in a brittle manner when loaded, especially under an impact force, and is prone to scratching compared to glass.

DURABILITY

Acrylic is a rigid thermoplastic with good resistance to UV. However its more rigid structure makes it susceptible to cracking when exposed to sudden impacts, and scratching of the surface. The melting point of acrylic is between 140°C and 170°C.

However, there are two common types of acrylic – cast acrylic and extruded acrylic. The properties of the two forms vary significantly and care should be taken to specify the type required for a specific application.

CAST ACRYLIC

This has a higher density and consequently is more resistant to scratching. However, this also means that cast acrylic is more likely to crack or shatter. It is generally used in locations where the possibility of impact is reduced and the scratch resistance is important. The melting point of is slightly higher (170°C) and the molten acrylic is more resistant and harder to form.

EXTRUDED ACRYLIC

This is sometimes referred to as impact-resistant acrylic sheet, and as this name suggests, it is used in applications where cast acrylic would shatter or chip. However, its surface is softer and is prone to scratching. The melting point of extruded acrylic (155°C) is lower and when molten it has better flow characteristics that make it suitable for moulding and forming.

HEALTH AND SAFETY

Combustion results in the release of carbon dioxide, water, methyl methacrylate and carbon monoxide. The quantity of carbon monoxide released will depend on the temperature and the amount of available oxygen, however this represents a toxic hazard and should be avoided.

The polishing and sanding of acrylic can create dust, and although this does not represent a toxic hazard, it is possible that quantities of the dust may irritate the respiratory system, so it is advisable to use a suitable dust mask and extraction, where possible.

COLOURS

Sheet acrylic is used in a wide range of applications, from sign-making to interior decoration. Consequently it is produced in a wide range of colours, from solid colours through to transparent, fluorescent, silk and frosted finishes.

Although this range of colours allows a significant degree of creativity for the jewellery designer, the reality is that it may be difficult to obtain materials of the desired colour and thickness in small quantities. Most suppliers or stockists carry a limited range of colours and thicknesses, which meet the needs of their regular customer base, but may be able to order non-stock colours.

A typical colour swatch supplied by a manufacturer of acrylic

However, with minimum order quantities and sheet sizes of up to 3 x 2 metres, a designer may be faced with purchasing large quantities of material, far beyond their requirements, in order to obtain a desired colour.

If this is multiplied by the number of colours that may be needed, the issue of cost, storage and handling may severely limit a designer's options in terms of colours and their ability to use materials efficiently.

In order to tackle this problem it advisable to identify a wide range of sources, from local sign-makers to distributors and manufacturers. Online auction sites also offer a range of materials; the prices per square metre may be much higher for small quantities, but this should be offset by the reduction in financial outlay for stock-holding on larger pieces.

MIRRORED ACRYLIC

There is a range of acrylic sheets that are produced with a mirrored surface. These were originally designed as an alternative to glass mirrors in applications where the impact strength of acrylic is a major advantage, e.g. exterior environments. Mirrored acrylic can be cut and machined in the same way as other grades of acrylic.

A range of coloured acrylic mirrors are available and include:

- silver
- gold
- bronze
- grey-black
- red
- orange
- yellow
- green
- sky blue
- purple
- double-sided and see-thru – two-way mirror.

ACRYLIC FINISHES

Standard acrylic sheets are available in solid colours, transparent clear and coloured sheets, opalescent, fluorescent, mirrored, frosted and silk surface finishes.

RECYCLING AND BIODEGRADABILITY

There is currently limited recycling of acrylic and this is usually in the form of industrial recycling where the material is re-ground and made into pellets for re-use. However this is at a relatively low level and most acrylic ends up in landfill sites where it only degrades at a slow rate. This is mainly because of the relative difficulty of recycling acrylic. It is possible to de-polymerise the resin but the process involves hazardous materials that can contaminate the recovered material. However, new technology may improve this process in the future.

Acrylic is listed under Plastics Recycling Symbol Number 7 – Plastics Other.

Other

nylon

Nylon is a generic name for a group of synthetic polymers known as polyamides. They were first produced in 1935 by DuPont and have grown to be one of the most common forms of plastic in use today. The polymer is generally produced in two forms – as fibres or as a solid plastic.

Nylon fibres are used in a wide range of applications, from textiles to rope and carpet fibre to the strings of musical instruments.

Solid nylon can be used for mechanical parts in applications that are not subject to excessive stress. Solid nylons are commonly extruded, cast or formed by injection moulding. The solid forms of nylon may be modified to enhance their strength, rigidity etc.

Nylons are thermoplastics and are generally transparent or translucent in their normal state. They exhibit a range of properties that can be used in jewellery design. These include:

- variety of finishes from dull to a lustrous shine
- high durability – even as a fine fibre
- resistance to abrasion
- high elongation before breaking
- resilience
- resistance to many chemicals.

The most common form of solid nylon is known as Nylon 6,6 (or Nylon 66): the name denotes the chemical structure of the polymer molecules and the chemical bonding within the polymer. Nylon 6,6 can be produced in either cast or extruded forms and with a variety of different additives and features, such as flame retardants. Therefore the properties of these materials differ and it is recommended that samples are tested before purchasing larger quantities for making jewellery.

For an overview of Nylon 6,6 variants please refer to:
http://www.matweb.com/Search/MaterialGroupSearch.aspx?GroupID=125

Nylon 6,6 exhibits additional properties:
- better resistance to weathering and sunlight degradation
- higher melting point (256°C)
- enhanced resistance to abrasion
- superior colour stability with less likelihood of yellowing.

DURABILITY

Nylon is generally resistant to chemicals, rot and fungal attack. However, the presence of strong acids results in hydrolysis that effectively depolymerises the molecules so that the material cracks and degrades; but this should not be an issue in jewellery applications.

HEALTH AND SAFETY

With the variety of polymers that are covered under the generic name 'nylon', it is only possible to generalise about the risks. Specific research should be conducted on the grade of nylon used, to determine what hazards may be associated with its use and disposal.

It should be noted that some nylons break down in a fire, producing smoke, fumes or ash that may contain hydrogen cyanide. Hydrogen cyanide is highly toxic and can cause death in under 60 seconds at sufficient concentration, therefore it is essential that any nylon residue is disposed of with care and not incinerated.

A sample of Nylon 6,6

COLOURS

One potential limitation of nylon is the lack of off-the-shelf colours, in most cases nylon is produced in natural, white or black. Therefore it must be dyed in order to achieve a range of colours; nylon 6,6 is more difficult to dye than other forms, due to its density and structure, however once the dyeing has been successfully achieved it will be stable and resistant to fading.

SURFACE FINISH

Nylon is generally available with either a gloss or matt surface finish.

RECYCLING AND BIODEGRADABILITY

There is currently limited recycling of nylon and it is usually in the form of industrial recycling where the material is re-ground and made into pellets for re-use. However, this is at a relatively low level and most nylon ends up in landfill sites where it only degrades at a slow rate. This is mainly because of the wide variety of nylon polymers and the range of colours produced, which makes it difficult to separate and recycle in economic quantities.

Nylons are listed under Plastics Recycling Symbol Number 7 – Plastics Other.

Other

polystyrene

Polystyrene is, in its pure state, a colourless, hard thermoplastic material with only limited flexibility. Now principally a derivative of petroleum, it was discovered in 1839 as an organic substance distilled from the resin of the *Liquidambar orientalis* tree that naturally polymerised on distillation. In the first half of the twentieth century it was realised that heating this material made it possible to produce larger molecules, which led to the development and naming of polystyrene.

Polystyrene went into production in 1939 with the development of a reactor vessel that helped to produce pelletised polystyrene.

Polystyrene is now one of the most widely used thermoplastics, with applications in packaging and as expanded polystyrene foam. However, the basic polystyrene polymer is often modified to produce co-polymers that have higher performance characteristics, for example ABS plastic (acrylonitrile butadiene styrene), which is used extensively in the electronics industry.

The most commonly available form of polystyrene sheet is commonly referred to as HIPS or high-impact polystyrene sheet.

DURABILITY

Polystyrene is a relatively hard polymer, providing limited flexibility. It shows a good resistance to some chemicals and solvents due to the stable nature of the polymer chains, but is particularly vulnerable to organic solvents. In particular it can be dissolved by products that contain acetone and by cyanoacrylate glues (superglues). Pure, unmodified polystyrene has poor resistance to UV radiation, which can cause yellowing and degradation, therefore it is generally not used in exposed environments.

Due to the rigid nature of polystyrene at room temperature, if the material is folded or bent sufficiently, the structure is damaged and micro-cracking of the polymer occurs, creating a permanent white mark in the material. If the bending is repeated the micro-cracking rapidly accelerates, with the material fracturing and failing. Therefore, unmodified polystyrene is not suitable for applications where there is the possibility of bending or deformation.

HEALTH AND SAFETY

High-temperature incineration of polystyrene produces mainly carbon dioxide, water and soot with some volatile compounds, however at lower temperatures it will produce carbon monoxide, styrene monomers and other polycyclic aromatic hydrocarbons which are known to be carcinogenic, mutagenic and teratogenic. Therefore it is not recommended that polystyrene should be disposed of by burning in a domestic environment.

In addition to the risks associated with burning polystyrene, it is also advisable to avoid breathing dust created while machining or sanding. Although polystyrene dust is not classified as toxic, it is always advisable to wear a suitable protective mask when working with any dust to avoid inhalation.

COLOURS

Polystyrene is available in a range of opaque colours, including red, orange, yellow, green, blue, black, white, brown, gold and silver.

Examples of polystyrene sheets

SURFACE FINISH
Polystyrene sheets are generally supplied with a gloss surface finish.

RECYCLING AND BIODEGRADABILITY
Polystyrene can be recycled, but due to its low value and the problems of recycling foamed forms, it is not commonly recycled and is not generally collected at roadside recycling points, however industrial recycling is increasing.

In addition to this polystyrene is not biodegradable (its lifetime is estimated as 500 years or more). This means that the majority of polystyrene waste will form landfill, where it will remain almost indefinitely. Added to this is the impact of foamed polystyrene, which is a serious pollutant in aquatic environments, where it floats on the surface and can travel vast distances.

Polystyrene is listed under Plastics Recycling Symbol Number 6.

Polyvinyl chloride (PVC)

PVC or polyvinyl chloride is a common thermoplastic and is widely used, mainly because of its relative cheapness and ease of assembly. It was discovered in the nineteenth century but it was not until the 1920s, when the basic polymer was modified with a plasticiser, that it became commercially usable. The pure PVC polymer tends to be rigid and relatively brittle, and so it is almost always modified, post-production, to improve its physical properties such as heat and UV resistance, plasticity and flame retardance. Therefore PVC is available in a wide range of forms and colours, from pipework to sheets and film.

DURABILITY

PVC is resistant to chemical and biological degradation and with the addition of plasticisers, it is more flexible and resistant to impact damage, making it a versatile material for construction applications etc.

HEALTH AND SAFETY

On combustion, PVC can release hydrogen chloride, which will dissolve in water to produce hydrochloric acid. In addition, the combustion of PVC releases dioxins (polychlorinated dibenzodioxins and dibenzofurans), which are known to bioaccumulate. These chemicals are mutagenic and carcinogenic and are therefore considered to be serious environmental pollutants and a risk to health.

Plasticisers used in the modification of PVC polymer, particularly diethylhexyl phthalate, have been cited as a possible hazard to human health, however the level of exposure in jewellery applications is probably insignificant.

The use of PVC cement in bonding releases solvents into the area adjacent to the material. Care should be taken to ensure sufficient ventilation. It is essential that the manufacturer's instructions and safety information are read and understood before using PVC cement.

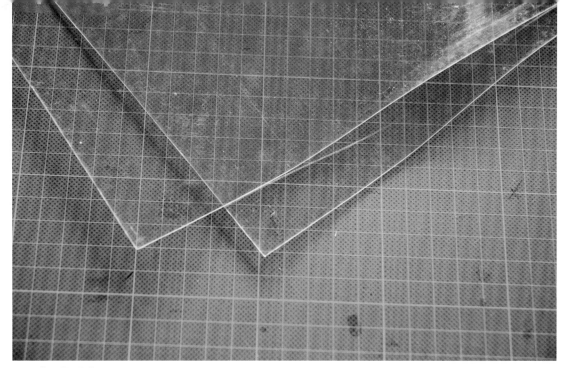

Examples of PVC sheets

COLOURS
PVC sheet is advertised for sale in a variety of colours, however most is clear, black or grey.

SURFACE FINISH
The surface finish is generally glossy, however clear PVC may appear to have a semi-gloss finish depending on the supplier.

RECYCLING AND BIODEGRADABILITY
PVC can be recycled, but due to the low cost of production and the relatively high cost of collection and reprocessing, recycling rates of PVC have been relatively low. However, legislation and new recycling methods are leading to a gradual increase in the recovery of PVC materials. PVC is not biodegradable, but remains in the environment. In addition to this problem, it has been suggested that PVC may leach chemicals into the groundwater, causing contamination and posing a health risk. Therefore the re-use or recycling of PVC should be encouraged.

PVC is listed under Plastics Recycling Symbol Number 3.

polyethylene

Polyethylene was first discovered in 1898 but did not reach industrial production until 1933. Since then, the process of polymerisation has been refined steadily to reduce cost and improve efficiency and consistency of the material produced.

Polyethylene-based thermoplastics form a group of plastics based on the ethylene monomer (a simple molecule consisting of two carbon atoms and four hydrogen atoms). However, the long basic polymer chain can be modified by the addition of branches, and the extent and type of these additions varies widely. Therefore, polyethylene can be divided into a number of sub-categories:

- ultra-high molecular weight polyethylene (UHMWPE)
- high molecular weight polyethylene (HMWPE)
- high-density polyethylene (HDPE)
- high-density cross-linked polyethylene (HDXLPE)
- cross-linked polyethylene (PEX)
- medium-density polyethylene (MDPE)
- linear low-density polyethylene (LLDPE)
- low-density polyethylene (LDPE)
- very low-density polyethylene (VLDPE)
- ultra-low molecular weight polyethylene (ULMWPE).

The most common forms of polyethylene are HDPE, LLDPE and LDPE.
HDPE is a polyethylene which has a low degree of branching and a higher tensile strength. It is commonly used in product packaging such as bottles and tubs, as well as water pipes. It accounts for 33% of all the polyethylene produced.

LLDPE is a mainly linear polymer with a significant number of short chain branches. It exhibits a higher tensile strength, impact and puncture resistance than LDPE. It is particularly suitable for producing thin films due to its flexibility, relative toughness and transparency. Therefore the majority of LLDPE is used for thin film production and is consumed in the packaging industry.

LDPE has polymers that have a high degree of branching with both long and short side chains. This reduces tensile strength but makes the material more ductile. The polymer structure does improve the processing and handling characteristics of the material, making it suitable for the production of rigid containers as well as film and sheet material.

DURABILITY
Polyethylene can be degraded by UV exposure.

HEALTH AND SAFETY
The combustion of polyethylene produces carbon dioxide, carbon monoxide and aldehydes as well as other by-products, depending on the type of polyethylene. Therefore it is not advisable to burn residual material and areas contaminated by smoke etc. should be ventilated thoroughly.

It is advisable to request the Material Safety Data Sheet from the supplier with any material purchased and to read and understand the potential hazards of working with the material.

COLOURS
Polyethylene is available in a wide range of colours, however for most industrial applications and thicknesses the colours are limited to black, white and transparent.

SURFACE FINISH
The surface finish of polyethylene will vary considerably with the polymer structure and samples should be obtained to assess suitability for purpose.

RECYCLING AND BIODEGRADABILITY
Polyethylene is recyclable, but significant quantities find their way into landfill where they will not degrade quickly. UV exposure does degrade polyethylene and there have been suggestions that bacteria may be effective at degrading it in a relatively short period of time, given the right environmental conditions, however this is not currently common practice.

LDPE is listed under Plastics Recycling Symbol Number 4.
HDPE is listed under Plastics Recycling Symbol Number 2.

thermoplastic plastics

The term 'thermoplastic' refers to plastics that melt when heated and solidify when cooled, rather than thermoset plastics, which, once formed cannot be melted by the application of heat.

In simple terms, thermoplastic plastics, like glass, exhibit a characteristic known as glass transition.[*] This is when the crystalline structure of a solid begins to break down and soften, with an increase in temperature. As the temperature rises, the internal bonds between molecules begin to break down and the nature of the material begins to change, becoming more pliable and flexible. As the temperature rises further, bonds break and the material will continue to soften until it reaches the point at which it becomes a liquid: the melting point.

This means that many plastics have three states – a crystalline solid, a 'gel phase' and a liquid state. The upper end of this gel phase is extremely useful when working with plastics as it allows the material to be moulded, stretched and formed. In addition to this, the surface of the plastic may become 'tacky' (because of the broken bonds between the molecules); this feature can be used to fuse two pieces of the same material together if they are heated sufficiently and then pressed together.

Material	Glass transition temperature[*]	Melting point[**]
Polypropylene	-10°c	173°c
Acrylic	85°c	160°c
Nylon 6,6	50°c	255°c
Polystyrene	100°c	240°c
PVC	85°c	240°c
Polyethylene	-78°c	100°c

[*]The glass transition temperature can be calculated in various ways, but the given temperature for a material is when the crystal structure has been reached and the material exhibits the coefficient of expansion of a crystalline solid.
[**]The melting point will vary depending on the exact formulation and figures are for guidance only.

The word 'plastic' derives from the Greek *plastikos*, meaning capable of being moulded or shaped. This characteristic is fundamentally important for anyone interested in working with plastics, and makes plastic an excellent medium for designers and jewellers.

damage and degradation

Although plastics are generally relatively resilient materials, there are a number of factors that can damage them, particularly when in sheet or filament form. The basic rule is that the finer the element the more susceptible it is to damage. For example, polypropylene sheet is available in thicknesses down to 280 microns (0.28 mm); at this thickness it is highly vulnerable to physical damage. Damage can be caused by the following factors.

CREASING

If a piece of flexible plastic is folded and pressed hard, the polymer structure will be damaged at the point of the highest stress. Some plastics will simply fail and crack or split along the line of greatest stress, while others will crease and leave a pale milky mark in the material which cannot be removed. The white mark, known as 'micro-cracking', is caused by a change in the molecular structure that alters the light absorption of the material, reflecting the light back.

COLD

If plastics are stored at low temperatures they should be allowed to acclimatise to room temperature (20°C) before scoring or creasing. At low temperatures they become brittle and may snap or shatter along a crease or score line.

HEAT

Although thermoplastics have a range of melting points, it is a fact that as the temperature increases the material begins to soften. If the temperature continues to rise, the plastic will begin to bend under its own weight and may become permanently deformed.

If the heat source is below the plastic, this may result in the plastic softening and sagging; it may then make contact with the heat source and melt. For example, if a piece of plastic jewellery is displayed in a cabinet lit with a halogen spotlight from below, the heat of the light will gradually soften it until it droops down onto the lamp, and melts.

UV EXPOSURE

Plastics vary in their resistance to UV light and some materials have UV stabilisers added to improve their resistance. UV radiation can cause yellowing and make the material brittle. It can also cause pigments in some plastics to fade and the colour can be lost over time. For example, polypropylene is liable to chain degradation from exposure to UV radiation, however in jewellery applications the level of UV exposure is unlikely to result in noticeable degradation.

LOADING

Rigid plastics, like acrylic, will withstand a degree of load stress, however as the load increases, the structure will begin to fracture. This may be observed as fine cracks or crazing of the material; it may also result in a sudden failure of the plastic and the piece will snap. The break will occur at a point of weakness, a score line or deep scratch, and may result in other cracks radiating out from the point of failure into the body of the material. Flexible plastics such as polypropylene are less likely to suffer from sudden failure and breaking, but if the loading is sufficient, the material will stretch and elongate, causing permanent damage and the eventual failure of the material.

Example of shattered acrylic

IMPACT DAMAGE

All plastics are vulnerable to impact damage. Rigid plastics will tend to crack, shatter or chip, whereas more flexible materials will stretch and distort at the point of impact.

Example of abraded acrylic

ABRASION

The range of abrasion resistance of different types of plastics is significant. Acrylic can easily be scratched and damaged by abrasion, whereas nylon materials are known for their resistance.

CHEMICAL ATTACK

Plastics exhibit different chemical resistance depending on their formulation, therefore it is advisable to check the resistance of the selected plastic if it is likely to come into contact with specific chemicals. For example, acrylic exhibits a generally poor resistance to solvents and will soften and even dissolve when exposed to some. However, it is unaffected by aqueous and alkaline solutions and dilute acids.

3 selecting materials

Examples of different plastics

rigid & brittle vs. soft & flexible

When selecting a type of plastic to meet design requirements, it is necessary to consider what properties are required in the finished piece – if the jewellery is designed to flex and move with the wearer, or is made from fine elements that will break if made from a rigid material, then a flexible plastic should be used. If the item is a robust form that must hold its shape, then a rigid plastic would be more suitable. The flexibility and strength of the polypropylene polymer, for example, makes even fine pieces strong and resilient.

colours & finishes

It is also important to select the material based on the colours and finishes available – if one plastic is only available in a limited selection of colours and cannot be dyed, then it may be necessary to select a different material that has similar properties but offers a wider selection of colours and finishes.

availability

Through experience, it has been learnt that some plastics are difficult to obtain and it may be impossible to obtain the desired material. In this situation, a designer may have to work with materials that are more readily available orseek other suppliers.

marking out patterns

The nature of most plastics and their resistance to chemicals is an advantage in the finished jewellery, making it durable and less likely to accumulate dirt and stains, however this also makes it difficult to mark out a design for cutting.

Most inks are designed for use on porous surfaces and therefore bead on the surface of plastics. They generally only dry very slowly and smudge when the material is handled. Permanent markers may be more effective, however once they are dry they may be more difficult to remove as they contain solvents which may have allowed the ink to penetrate the surface.

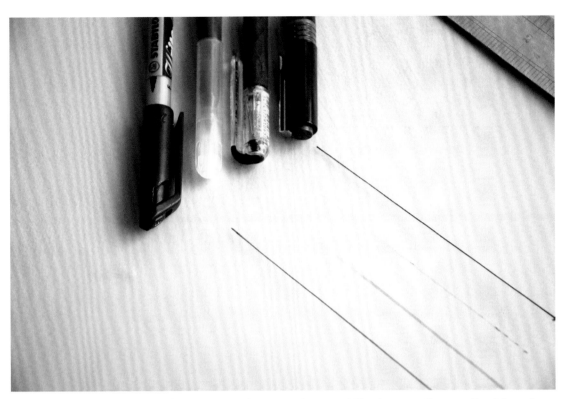

Marking out on plastic From left to right: permanent marker – cannot be removed; fibre tip pen – easily removed by wiping surface; gel pen – easily removed by wiping surface; Rotring pen – once dried, only removed with soap and water.

Rotring Isographic pens provide an ideal drawing medium: the pens deliver a fine, accurate line and the ink dries relatively quickly. Once dry, the ink does not smudge easily and when the design has been cut it can be washed from the surface with a solution of soap and water, leaving the surface clear of marks.

See: http://www.rotring.com/en/8-isograph

Rotring ink is available in four colours, but the black and white ink will allow a design to be drawn on all of the colours of plastic available.

See: http://www.rotring.com/en/10-inks-and-accessories

Marking out a pattern prior to cutting

Rotring inks

5 cutting plastics

cutting plastic by hand

The method of cutting plastic will depend on the thickness and flexibility or rigidity of the material. Thin and flexible plastics can be cut using methods similar to those used for thin card, whereas the cutting of thicker and rigid plastics is similar to cutting aluminium or fine-grained wood.

CUTTING FLEXIBLE SHEET PLASTIC – FOR EXAMPLE 500 MICRON POLYPROPYLENE SHEETS

TIN SNIPS

A pair of jeweller's fine tin snips that have been sharpened and tightened specifically for the purpose will allow the manual cutting of fine and detailed patterns in polypropylene sheet of 500 microns (800 micron sheet can be cut in this way, but it is hard on the hands). If the snips are correctly sharpened they will cut an accurate, square edge.

Cutting with tin snips

SCISSORS

Scissors can be used to cut polypropylene, however they must be of sufficient quality and sharpness to cut cleanly though the sheets without tearing, which would give a ragged and poor-quality finish. Any small nicks and marks on the blade will also mark the cut edge of the material.

The disadvantage of using scissors is that they do not allow the accuracy and fine control that an experienced person can exert with a set of sharp tin snips, particularly when it comes to fine details and cutting long filaments.

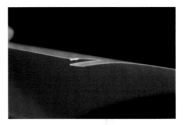

Close-up of a poor cut with blunt scissors

SCALPEL

A traditional artist's scalpel is an accurate and clean way of cutting 280–800 micron polypropylene sheets and is particularly effective when cutting fine internal details that would be difficult to cut using tin snips or scissors.

Cutting with a scalpel

CUTTING INTERMEDIATE PLASTIC SHEETS – FOR EXAMPLE 1 MM POLYSTYRENE SHEETS

CRAFT KNIFE

Polystyrene sheets can be cut using a sharp craft knife, however it may be necessary to repeat the cut several times in order to cut through the material. This gives a clean cut without discolouration to the body of the plastic.

Cutting with a craft knife

SCORING AND BREAKING

If the surface is scored once and the polystyrene is then folded to fracture the material along the score line, the result is a cut that shows micro-cracking of the fractured material in the form of white stress fractures.

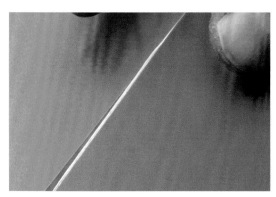

Discolouration of plastic edge from cutting

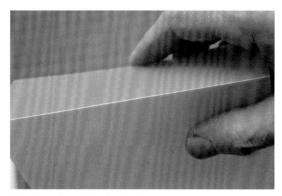

Discolouration of plastic edge from scoring

TIN SNIPS AND SCISSORS

The use of shearing scissors or cutters can cause the polymer to 'tear' along the cut with the result that micro-cracks occur along the cut line. This produces white discolouration in the material.

JEWELLER'S PIERCING SAW

For cutting thicker sheets of polystyrene, a jeweller's piercing saw, fitted with a fine blade, can be effective.

Sawing polystyrene

PRECIOUS JEWELLERY FROM PLASTICS

CUTTING RIGID PLASTICS – FOR EXAMPLE 4 MM ACRYLIC

SCORING AND BREAKING

For acrylic sheets of 1–3 mm it is possible to break large pieces by scoring a straight line across one face of the acrylic with a Stanley knife and then placing this over an edge and applying pressure to both sides of the score line, causing the acrylic to crack along the scored line. With thicker sheets of 4–5 mm it may be necessary to score both sides deeply, in order to ensure that the crack follows the scored line along its full length.

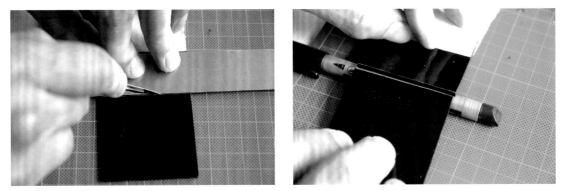

Scoring and cracking acrylic

It may be possible to score and crack sheets thicker than 5 mm, but it becomes increasingly difficult and alternative methods may be more effective.

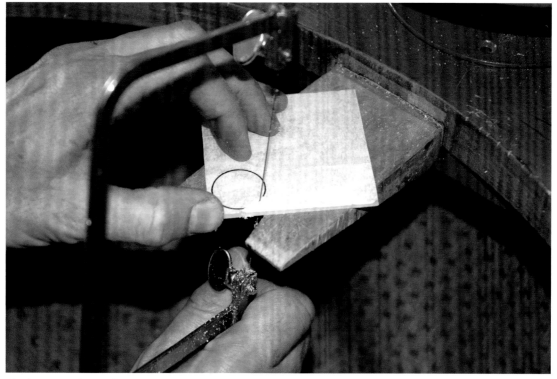

Piercing saw cutting acrylic

JEWELLER'S PIERCING SAW

For fine work it is possible to use a jeweller's piercing saw to cut the delicate or complex details. In this case it is necessary to select the correct blade for the thickness of material – a medium blade for thicknesses of 1–5 mm and a coarse blade for thicker material.

One problem that arises with this method of cutting, is that both the material and blade heat up with the friction generated during the cutting, and fine particles of acrylic dust can become melted onto the blade, binding with the material that is being cut and causing the blade to jam in the work. If the heat is sufficient, the blade will be effectively welded into the material and cannot be removed. It is then necessary to cut around the blade and file it out of the plastic.

This problem can easily be avoided if the piece is covered on both sides with masking tape: the tape causes the fine particles of acrylic to release from the teeth of the saw blade and there is less chance of the blade sticking in the work.

QUICK REFERENCE GUIDE TO CUTTING PLASTICS BY HAND

Plastic	Tin snips	Scissors	Scalpel
Flexible plastic (up to 2 mm)	High quality cut on material of up to 800 microns	Good quality results up to 800 microns	Detailed cutting up to 500 microns
Intermediate plastics (up to 2 mm)	Plastics may exhibit micro-cracking discolouration along edges	Plastics may exhibit micro-cracking discolouration along edges	Good-quality results up to 1–1.5 mm, depending on material
Rigid plastic (up to 1.5 mm)	May cause micro-cracking or splintering on edges, depending on material	May cause micro-cracking or splintering on edges, depending on material	Multiple passes may be required, so of limited value

Plastic	Craft knife	Scoring and breaking	Jeweller's piercing saw
Flexible plastic (up to 5 mm)	For cutting up to 2 mm	Flexible plastics will only break with difficulty and edges show micro-cracking discolouration	Only effective on material over 2 mm
Intermediate plastics (up to 5 mm)	Good-quality results up to 2.5 mm, depending on material	Plastics will break but edges may exhibit micro-cracking discolouration	Highly accurate for detailed cutting over 1 mm thickness
Rigid plastic (up to 5 mm)	Multiple passes may be required, but generally more effective than scalpel	Highly effective if scored sufficiently	Highly accurate for detailed cutting

cutting plastics with power tools

There are several alternative power tools that can be used for cutting thicker plastic boards, including:

▶ band saw
▶ circular saw
▶ power hacksaw
▶ spiral saw.

BAND SAW

There is a wide range of sizes from industrial to hobby band saws that are capable of cutting thick plastic sheet, however a number of factors affect their performance:

- They must be fitted with an appropriate blade that will cut the plastic but not clog. (Consult the supplier for an appropriate specification.)
- The thicker the plastic, the harder it is to cut and a more powerful motor will be required. Hobby machines will cut up to 5 mm but may struggle with material of 5 mm and above.
- Most band saws have two wheels – this reduces the wear and bending of the blade and increases blade life. Hobby machines may have three smaller wheels, but the blades are consequently thinner and cutting will be more difficult and less accurate.
- The speed and length of the blade may also affect cutting: if friction makes the blade too hot, plastic particles will stick to the blade and cause it to clog and jam. Longer blades will have more time to cool and will perform better.

Band saw cutting acrylic

CIRCULAR SAW

Either a bench saw or a hand-held circular saw can be used to cut plastic. The power of the motor and thickness of the blade make these machines effective at cutting blocks of at least 30 mm thickness.

However, the blades tend to be designed for heavy-duty cutting and the resulting edge of the plastic is rough and requires significant work to smooth and finish it.

Circular saw cutting acrylic

POWER HACKSAW

These are readily available and inexpensive and therefore offer a cost-effective option for cutting large sheets of material. Blades should be selected that are suitable for the material and thickness. (Refer to manufacturer or distributor for details.)

These saws can be used to cut simple curves and shapes in plastic boards. However, due to the vibration that the cutting action produces, they may cause rigid and brittle plastics to crack or splinter.

Power hacksaw cutting acrylic

SPIRAL SAW

These are a relatively recent development and use a spiral blade to cut in any direction within the material. As they produce very little vibration, they offer an effective way to cut complex shapes with minimal risk of cracking and splintering.

However, the blades remove a relatively wide channel of material (approximately 3 mm), making it difficult to produce intricate designs on a small scale. In addition, the saws are comparatively expensive and although they represent a good investment for large-scale production, they are less justifiable for smaller businesses.

Spiral saw cutting acrylic

QUICK REFERENCE GUIDE TO CUTTING PLASTICS USING POWER TOOLS

Plastic	Band saw	Circular saw*	Power hacksaw*	Spiral saw*
Flexible plastic (over 2 mm)	May clog blade, ensure correct blade is used	Only suitable for use on materials over 5 mm	Only suitable for use on materials over 3 mm	Accurate cutting but only suitable for use on materials over 3 mm
Intermediate plastics (over 1.5 mm)	May clog blade, ensure correct blade is used	Only suitable for use on materials over 5 mm	Only suitable for use on materials over 3 mm	Accurate cutting but only suitable for use on materials over 3 mm
Rigid plastic (over 1.5 mm)	May clog blade, ensure correct blade is used	Only suitable for use on materials over 5 mm	Cuts well but vibration may cause cracking and splintering	Accurate cutting but only suitable for use on materials over 3 mm

*Maximum cut depth depending on blade length and motor rating of power tool.

HEALTH AND SAFETY

Power tools can cause serious injury and manufacturers' instructions should be read, understood and guidelines followed. Suitable protective clothing should be worn.

cutting plastics on industrial equipment

A number of industrial processes can be used to cut plastics where larger-scale production is required. These range from small machines that are only slightly bigger than those designed for hobby use, to computer-guided industrial machines that can process 2.5 x 3.5 metre sheets of plastic, in thicknesses of over 60 mm.

LASER CUTTING

A laser cutter uses a focused beam of light to 'burn' through the material being cut. The power of the laser generates a beam that has sufficient energy to vaporise the material and even cut through thick plastics. However, the plastic surrounding the cut is subjected to localised heating which may cause the edge of the plastic to liquefy temporarily, creating a rounded, slightly thickened edge.

The power and speed of the laser cutter head's movement will impact on the quality of the cut, so it is advisable to consult a specialist company and request that samples are tested for accuracy and quality before placing an order or purchasing a laser cutter.

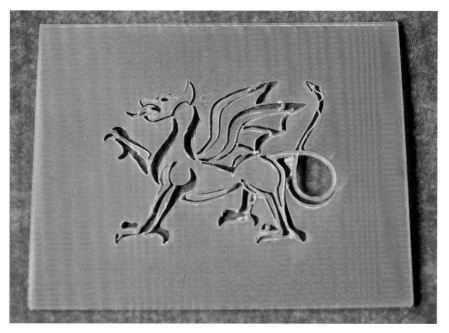

Sample of laser cut polypropylene

WATER-JET CUTTING

Water-jet cutting machines use a focused, high-pressure water jet, with or without a cutting aggregate, to blast through the material that is being cut. With sufficiently high pressure and water flow, they can cut steel and concrete.

One advantage of water-jet cutting is that the process does not produce any heat, so there is no possibility of the surrounding material melting. However, the nature of the plastic polymer can affect the cutting process: in general, the longer the polymer chains and the more flexible the plastic, the more likely it is for the plastic to 'feather' when cut, leaving the edge rough and giving a poor finish. This is because the polymer resists the water jet and will not cut cleanly, the polymer breaks away from the edge in short fibres that remain partly connected to the edge.

ROUTERS AND MILLING MACHINES

These machines use vertically orientated spindles known as routers or cutters that protrude from the machine table or from an overhead, computer-controlled platform and can be spun at speeds typically between 3000 and 24,000 rpm. The material may be passed through the machine or the cutter may be guided over the surface where the cutters mould a profile into it.

These machines are commonly used on thicker plastics where a complex three-dimensional shape is required, rather than a simple profile.

CUTTING PLASTICS ON INDUSTRIAL EQUIPMENT

Plastic	Laser cutting*	Water-jet cutting	Routing/milling machine**
Polypropylene	Material adjacent to the cut edge melts and forms a thickened, beaded edge	Edges exhibit feathering and material does not cut cleanly	Polypropylene swarf can stick to cutters and makes machining difficult
Acrylic	Clean, high-quality cut	Good cutting performance	Use cast acrylic for best results
Nylon	Good cutting performance	Good cutting performance	Excellent for machining
Polystyrene	Fair cutting performance, some melting of edge	Good cutting performance	Suitable for machining
PVC	PVC liberates hydrogen chloride gas which is hazardous and should be avoided.	Can be cut with water-jet cutter	Suitable for machining
Polyethylene	Material adjacent to the cut edge may be discoloured – white PVC will discolour to tan. Material adjacent to the cut edge melts and forms a thickened, beaded edge. Yellowish deposits must be cleaned away from cut edges after cutting. May release toxic fumes when laser cut.	Relative hardness compared to polypropylene means that polyethylene exhibits a cleaner cut	Suitable for machining

*Since laser-cutting plastics produces fine particulate matter and gases that may be inhaled, suitable extraction and filtration are required to ensure a safe working environment. It is essential to consult the manufacturer regarding the safe use of laser cutters on a particular material.
**Suitable for thicker material only.

---

6 joining plastics

adhesives

The process of adhesion requires mechanical and/or chemical action, the attraction of charged molecules, the creation of an electrostatic charge or the diffusion of material across the joint. Adhesives that bond plastics can be divided into three main types.

Epoxy adhesive

K&S Magnumbond

Super Glue

CHEMICAL ADHESIVES

Examples include superglues (cyanoacrylates) and epoxy adhesives which bond to the surfaces of the materials being joined. When the adhesive cures it holds the two surfaces together. The cure mechanisms vary depending on the type of adhesive, and the different chemical formulations of adhesives bond more or less effectively to different plastics.

HEALTH AND SAFETY

It is recommended that when any adhesive (or equipment) is used that the manufacturer's product safety data sheets are read, understood and followed.

Hot-melt adhesive

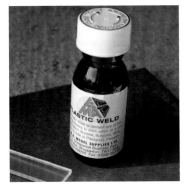

Plastic Weld

THERMAL ADHESIVES

These include hot-melt adhesives, which are applied at temperatures up to 200°C (cool-melt adhesives are used at lower temperatures: 50–70°C). Hot-melt adhesives are in themselves thermoplastics of various formulations and when heated until they are liquid, they exhibit adhesive properties. As the material cools it solidifies and holds the two surfaces together.

In addition to the adhesive nature of the molten material, the heat transferred to the plastic by the hot melt softens the plastic and improves the adhesion between the plastic and hot melt.

SOLVENTS

Solvents act not as a bond between two surfaces but more like a 'catalyst' that helps them fuse together. A solvent is applied to the surfaces of the plastics and dissolves the top layers to be joined. The liquidised surfaces are then brought together and they fuse and join. The solvent then evaporates and the liquefied material solidifies, leaving the two surfaces fused together.

selecting an adhesive

Just as the polymer structures of different types of plastic are radically different, so are the adhesives required to bond them. It is not possible to generalise about adhesives for all plastics and it is necessary to deal with each type of plastic individually.

With some plastics available in a wide variety of forms, it is advisable to thoroughly test the adhesives selected with the chosen material. The adhesive should be applied, the surface joined and then the adhesive allowed to cure, cool or evaporate thoroughly. The resulting bond should then be tested for strength and durability.

bonding polypropylene

The structure of polypropylene provides limited mechanical adhesion, its high chemical resistance limits chemical adhesion and there is little evidence to suggest that the other forms of adhesion are in operation.

The result is that most adhesives applied to the surface of polypropylene exhibit poor wetting qualities when liquid and, once dry, they easily peel away from the surface and fail to adhere. This can clearly be seen with most superglues and other commonly available adhesives. However, two forms of adhesive have been found to be effective.

Gap filling with hot-melt

HOT-MELT ADHESIVE

When liquid hot-melt adhesive is applied to the surface of sheet polypropylene, heat is transferred to the polypropylene and the material is softened. The adhesive properties are improved and the hot-melt bonds to the surfaces. However, the type of hot-melt (formulations differ between manufacturers) and the temperature of application can affect the bond, so it is necessary to test a sample before assembling any jewellery.

In some cases the adhesion between two sheets of polypropylene may be poor and the sheets can be separated, leaving the adhesive on one surface. In applications where the holt-melt is used to fill a gap and the polypropylene is then pushed into the hot glue, the adhesion can be effective enough to create a durable piece of jewellery because the shearing force necessary to break the bond between the hot-melt and polypropylene cannot be applied.

When bonding translucent polypropylene, it is possible to see the hot-melt between the layers of material. Therefore the designer should ensure that the bonded areas are suitably covered for aesthetic purposes.

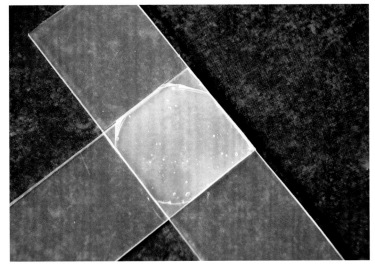

Hot-melt between translucent sheets

HEALTH AND SAFETY

Hot-melt adhesives present some difficulties in application: the temperature of the hot melt means that fine work is difficult to handle and care must be taken to avoid skin contact with the hot adhesive.

K+S VIELZWECKKLEBER/MAGNUMBOND

This is a fast-hardening, single-component cyanogen acrylate adhesive. The generic name 'cyanoacrylate' includes superglues. However, the formulation of cyanogen acrylate adhesives may be based on methyl 2-cyanoacrylate, ethyl-2-cyanoacrylate, n-butyl cyanoacrylate or 2-octyl cyanoacrylate, or a mixed composition. Consequently, different formulations of superglue will exhibit different properties.

In the case of K+S Vielzweckkleber/Magnumbond the formulation has been found to bond effectively with polypropylene and a range of other materials.

The adhesive requires some moisture to cure. The natural humidity in the air is usually sufficient for this process, however skin contact provides a source of moisture and causes the adhesive to polymerise rapidly. Therefore, application of the adhesive is best achieved directly from the container or using an inert material, such as a stiff piece of wire.

HEALTH AND SAFETY

Cyanoacrylates are not considered to be toxic, however some people may become sensitised by repeated exposure. In addition to this, these adhesives can bond skin quickly and effectively, therefore care should be taken during application to avoid skin contact.

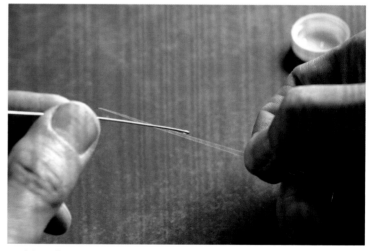

Applying adhesive

The adhesive should be stored in a sealed container to avoid moisture causing it to cure, and as temperature accelerates the curing process, unused adhesive may be kept in a refrigerator.

bonding acrylic

Acrylic can be bonded with either an adhesive or a solvent: both processes produce a strong bond. However, the choice of bonding should relate to the application in which it will be used. With some forms of transparent acrylic it may be possible to see the bond through the material and therefore it is advisable to test the different processes on scrap material before assembling the final piece of jewellery.

ADHESIVES

There are a number of adhesives that will bond acrylic to metal and other rigid surfaces. Readily available types include:

- superglues (cyanoacrylate-based adhesives)
- epoxy adhesives
- hot-melt adhesives.

In addition to these adhesives, solvents can be used to bond acrylic, for example Plastic Weld.

SUPERGLUES

Based on acrylate molecules, these adhesives are fast drying, easy to apply and provide a strong bond. However, caution should be taken to avoid contact with the skin. (See manufacturer's instructions before use.)

The resulting bond with superglue can be broken by a shearing force (force from the side) that causes the bond to fracture. Jewellery designs should take this into consideration and the piece should be protected or supported against shearing forces.

HEALTH AND SAFETY

Care should be taken with solvents and the manufacturer's instructions should be observed at all times.

EPOXY ADHESIVES

These are generally supplied as a two-part material (base and hardener) that are mixed prior to use and set through a chemical reaction within the adhesive. Epoxy adhesives are available in a range of finishes and care should be taken to select a material that does not show through the acrylic when cured.

Epoxy bonds tend to take longer to cure, but may provide a stronger bond and are more resistant to high temperatures.

Both types of adhesive are generic and formulations will vary from manufacturer to manufacturer. It is advised that any adhesive tested thoroughly on samples before use on final pieces, to ensure that the bond strength is sufficient and the colour and finish appropriate to the application.

HOT-MELT ADHESIVE

The application of hot-melt adhesive between two sheets of acrylic gives a strong and resistant bond, however it is recommended that the combination of the type of acrylic being used and the particular brand of hot-melt adhesive should be tested before making final pieces.

PLASTIC WELD

An alternative to the use of adhesives is the use of a solvent that liquefies both surfaces of the acrylic to be bonded and then, once the piece has been assembled, the solvent evaporates and the acrylic surfaces solidify and are 'welded' together.

An example of this is EMA Plastic Weld, which is supplied in a liquid form and can be applied to the surface of the acrylic with a brush. On contact with the acrylic, the solvent breaks down the acrylic polymers and the surface becomes sticky and appears to be melting. As Plastic Weld is highly volatile it evaporates rapidly, and as it does so the acrylic polymers reform across the boundary of the assembled pieces.

bonding nylon

ADHESIVES

Unlike polypropylene, nylon is generally considered to be bondable. Nylon can be bonded to itself and to other substrates without significant preparations, however light abrasion can improve adhesion.

Recommended adhesives include nylon-phenolic, nitrile-phenolic, nitriles, neoprene, modified epoxy, cyanoacrylate (superglue), modified phenolic and polyurethane.[1]

Examples of suitable adhesives include:
- Araldite® 2040 Gray, Flexible

General-purpose polyurethane adhesive with a 15-minute work life. It cures at room temperature, and is suitable for use with nylon and other plastics.
- Joiner's Mate Adhesive 310 ml

Suitable for use with most materials, especially metals and plastics. Clear, one-part, moisture-curing adhesive. High grab strength within 5 minutes. Good for vertical joints. Water resistant, Class D4.

SOLVENTS

There are solvents that will dissolve nylon, for example formic acid, however these materials are very toxic and corrosive and are therefore not suitable for use.

1 Arthur Landrock, *Adhesives Technology Handbook*, Noyes Publications, 1985, p. 195

bonding polystyrene

ADHESIVES

Polystyrene can be bonded with one-part, moisture-cured, polyurethane wood glues. However, the availability of a solvent for polystyrene means that polyurethane adhesives are mainly used for expanded polystyrene bonding applications.

SOLVENTS

Frequently referred to as polystyrene cement, methyl ethyl ketone is used as a solvent that dissolves a small amount of the plastic until it evaporates, leaving the parts fused. This adhesive is commonly used for assembling model kits and is therefore readily available from model shops and craft outlets. Humbrol Standard Polystyrene Cement is widely available from model shops and online suppliers.

HOT-MELT ADHESIVES

Hot-melt adhesives do provide a strong bond when used with polystyrene. However, it is recommended that the combination of the type of polystyrene being used and the particular brand of hot-melt adhesive should be tested together before making final pieces.

bonding PVC

PVC can be bonded using PVC cements, available from plumbing suppliers etc. PVC cement is commonly a blend of tetrahydrofuran, butanone and cyclohexanone, all solvents that are known to dissolve PVC polymer and liquefy the surfaces, allowing them to fuse together.

PVC cements should be applied to the surfaces to be bonded and the surfaces then pressed firmly together before the solvents evaporate. This allows the surfaces to fuse and solidify as the solvent evaporates.

HOT-MELT ADHESIVES

Hot-melt adhesives did not provide a suitable plastic-to-plastic bond when used with PVC.

bonding polyethylene

Polyethylene is difficult to bond due to its structure and high resistance to solvents. Adhesion can be improved by heat-treating the surface prior to the application of adhesives, but even in this case the bond is relatively weak. Consequently, the main form of adhesion in most applications is achieved by the localised melting of the material and the fusing of the molten elements or via mechanical fastenings.

Polyethylene can be fused using hot-gas welding, ultrasonic welding, laser welding and infrared welding, however these techniques are not generally available in the jewellery studio.

HOT-MELT ADHESIVE
Hot-melt adhesives did not provide a suitable plastic-to-plastic bond when used with polyethylene.

mechanical fixing

Due to the difficulties associated with adhesion to some plastics and the limited number of adhesives available, a practical method of joining components together or to other materials is the use of mechanical fixing.

FLEXIBLE PLASTICS

RIVETING
A wide range of rivets is available in a variety of materials, but most are designed for industrial applications and may not be suitable for jewellery applications. They may be too large, of unsuitable aesthetic appearance or made of an inappropriate material, but this will depend on the individual design and application.

However, it is possible to locate rivets in very small sizes, for example solid rivets down to 1.59 mm or less. In addition there are some types of rivet that are produced for more aesthetic purposes, for example the double cap rivets used on many leather goods.

If precious-metal rivets are required, it is possible to fabricate these from rods or tubes to replicate the traditional forms available. In this case it is possible to produce the size and type of rivet that is most appropriate to the design requirements.

When applying rivets it is important to remember that they are fixed by applying considerable force to deform the rivet. Therefore, fine and delicate materials may be subjected to forces that crush and spread them, distorting the final piece. It is advisable that all riveting methods are tested on scrap material prior to the application in the finished work.

The use of an appropriate washer under the rivet is an important consideration as it helps to reduce the stresses applied in fixing the rivet and also reduces the chance that the rivet will pull out of the plastic.

Materials: 0.7 mm silver discs, silver tube

Fabricated silver tube rivet and silver washer

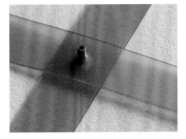
Tube rivet inserted through plastics

Washer placed over rivet

Making and fixing tube rivets in polypropylene

Centre punch used to fix rivet

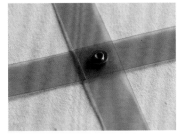
Finished rivet

Cutting a screw thread

SCREW FITTINGS

Where riveting is impractical or may damage a design, a practical alternative may be to use a screw fitting that can be tightened by hand.

One problem with using screw fittings is that for most jewellery applications normal fittings do not have a suitable appearance. However, a solution is to use fittings from the body-piercing market. These are made of high-grade surgical steel and are manufactured in a variety of sizes and styles.

The manufacturers of these fittings use a standard thread size for their pieces and it is possible to buy the individual parts direct from the manufacturers. By requesting the relevant thread cutter, a length of threaded bar can be made from a suitable gauge of silver wire (1.6 mm for a thread cutter M 1.6 x 0.35 made from HSS (high-speed steel)).

The bar can then be cut to any length and can either be soldered directly onto a small base plate, or a threaded ball can be attached to either end. By adding a small amount of superglue to the screw threads they can be permanently sealed, creating a durable fixing though several layers of the plastic.

Centre punching the back plate

STAPLING

In the same way that paper can be securely fastened with staples, it is possible to staple thin sheets of plastic. Rather than using a conventional stapler and staples, which do not match the aesthetics of jewellery, precious-metal wire can be used.

Drilling the back plate

Cutting a thread into the back plate

Checking the thread fit

Threaded bar soldered to the fitting

Making screw fittings

The front and back plates

Finished fitting

Two or more pieces of plastic can be fixed by assembling them into their positions and then two holes can be made, either with a fine drill bit or with a hot wire. A piece of wire is then folded into a flat U shape and passed through the holes. Once in place, the whole piece should be placed on a firm surface and the wire can be bent down to securely fasten the material.

Materials: silver wire, plastic

Marking out the staple holes

Assembled plastic with silver cut to length and holes drilled

Silver folded to form staple

Staple inserted and one side folded out

Folding out staple with pliers

Pressing down staple with pliers

Securing the staple

Finished fitting

Stitching a polypropylene ruff

STITCHING

Just as textiles can be stitched, it is possible to stitch fine plastic sheets together or to other materials.

Even with polypropylene at 280 microns in thickness, it is still difficult to sew directly through the sheets and therefore it is necessary to mark out and pre-drill or melt the holes to ensure both accuracy and an aesthetic finish.

Depending on the thread used, it may be preferable to make the holes using a heated point. This produces holes that do not have sharp edges, which could result in the threads wearing and breaking over time.

SLOTTING AND CLIPPING

It is possible to secure thicker sheet plastics effectively without the need for adhesive or mechanical fixings of any form. By cutting a slot into the material, another tabbed piece can be passed through the slot and, if designed correctly, will lock into the slot and cannot easily be withdrawn. This principle can be adapted and modified in many ways, from single slots securing the ends of an element to multiple interlocking parts. This principle is best used when the parts involved are under opposing tension, as the tension helps to maintain the form of the design and ensure that the fixing points remain secure.

The slot must be cut to two-thirds of the width of the tabbed piece that will be inserted through it. The end of the tabbed piece is cut in a curve that facilitates the tab passing through the slot and then two cuts or notches are made, one on either side of the tabbed piece and one third of the width of the material. The tab can then be slipped into the slot on the first piece of material, slipped to one side and the other side of the tab can be pushed through the slot. Once the tab is in place it can be slipped back to the middle of the slot and it cannot then be withdrawn unless it is first moved to one side.

Pieces that use this form of construction require careful design. If the principles can be mastered it is possible to construct complex and dramatic forms as shown in the examples on page 63.

Slot (blue) and tab (red)

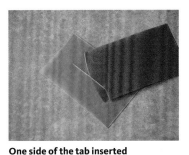
One side of the tab inserted

Inserting the second side
Slot and tab

Tab is secured in slot

In the example, the piece is constructed from a small hexagon of polypropylene, with six strips fixed into place using the tab-and-slot principle. Slots are then cut at intervals, evenly along each strip and the strips are threaded through the slots in a symmetrical pattern. The result is a complex pattern of intertwined strips.

The same basic structure can be used to create numerous different forms and shapes, depending on where the slots are cut and which strip is threaded through.

Similar principles are used in origami and other forms of paperfolding, and these methods can be used as inspiration for an almost infinite variety of designs.

Front
Slot and tab examples

Rear

A similar result can be obtained by cutting two pieces of plastic and making a cut on each piece that is halfway through the material; the pieces can then be slipped together to form an interlocking pattern. However, this is not as secure as the slot-and-tab method. So when designing work using this method, it is important to ensure that the pieces cannot slip apart.

Example of side slotting

ATTACHING BEADING

If fine elements are cut or strands of polypropylene are used, it is possible to secure beads along the length or at the ends. However, the application of an adhesive may be insufficient to secure the beads and additional, mechanical support may be required.

In this case the beads should be threaded onto the filament and a small quantity of adhesive applied where the beads are to be secured. The end of the filament can then be heated and pressed into the end bead.

Sliding bead onto filament

Apply adhesive

Melting the end of the filament
Attaching beads

Pressing the molten plastic into the bead

HEAT FUSION

As many plastics have a relatively low melting point, it is possible to join elements by heating them carefully until they begin to melt. If two pieces are placed together at this point the materials will begin to fuse and bond.

However, the technique is difficult to control as the material will begin to distort under the application of heat, and will stretch and break if it is not carefully controlled. These factors make it difficult to fuse small elements without damaging them, therefore the technique may have limited use in jewellery-making.

Example of heat fusion

NB

The welding process described here is based on the manufacturer's guidance. Although it has been observed in use with ABS plastic by the author, the process described is not the result of direct experience of ultrasonic welding in conjunction with polypropylene, due to the high cost of the equipment required.

Examples of bolts, pins and rivets

ULTRASONIC WELDING

The basic principle of ultrasonic assembly is the conversion of electrical energy through a converter, which then expands and contracts at the same frequency, converting the electrical energy into high-frequency mechanical vibration. This vibration is amplified by a booster and then transferred to the work piece through a shaped tool called a horn. Parts being assembled are clamped together under moderate pressure, at which point ultrasonic vibrations force the parts to collide against each other at a preset frequency, creating a molecular bond equal to or above the material strength of the parts.

RIGID PLASTICS

MECHANICAL FIXINGS

As with most resistant materials, a wide range of mechanical fixings can be used to assemble components. For example acrylic can be cut, shaped and formed in similar ways to wood and metal, then many of the methods of fixing these materials can be applied. Methods of fixing can include:

- bolts/pins/rivets
- setting
- links
- sewing.

BOLTS/PINS/RIVETS

All of these methods can be employed simply by drilling a pilot hole through the piece and using a suitable fixing. It is possible to fabricate these fixings in silver so that they blend with the jewellery design, or to create a more industrial appearance by using small versions of conventional fixings.

However, consideration must be given to the relative brittleness of the material, in particular cast acrylic, where excess pressure resulting from over-tightening mechanical fixings or riveting can cause cracking or fracturing around the fixing hole. This problem can be acute in fine materials and alternative methods should be employed in order to obviate this problem.

SETTING

In many respects rigid plastics are similar to amber in hardness, scratch resistance and processing and, where amber can be cabochon cut and set in jewellery, it is possible to accomplish a similar result with plastics such as acrylic. Care should be taken when setting acrylic in order to avoid scratching the surface around the setting itself, as it may be difficult to remove scratches once the piece has been set.

Materials: 0.7 mm silver discs, silver rod

Fabricated silver rivet and silver washer

Rivet inserted through plastics

Washer placed over rivet
Making and fixing solid rivets in acrylic

Hammering over the rivet

Finished rivet

Example of set acrylic

LINKS

Perhaps the simplest method of joining pieces of acrylic is the use of links. If the pieces are designed so that they accommodate holes at the edges, then silver links can be inserted and the pieces can be incorporated into a chain of some kind.

Care should be taken to ensure that the links do not exert excess pressure on the plastic, as this will inevitably lead to fracturing around the holes and failure in the jewellery.

Linked acrylic elements

It is also possible to link elements with stainless steel wire. Using wire of 0.8–1 mm, a hole can be drilled to fit the wire; one end of the wire can be inserted into the hole and bonded in using a suitable adhesive or solvent. If the process is repeated with the other end of the wire onto a second acrylic element, the two pieces can be linked.

The stainless steel can be preformed to produce elegant curves and linking pieces to form chains or more abstract designs.

Drilling the hole for the wire

Applying adhesive to the wire

Wire inserted into hole
Linking with wires

Second piece attached

SEWING

It is possible to attach elements together using conventional sewing techniques, if holes are pre-drilled into the pieces. However, as with sewing any rigid material it is essential to ensure that any edges that come into contact with the thread are carefully rounded and prepared to ensure that they do not wear the threads. In addition to this it is important to ensure that the selected thread will not stretch over time and that it is strong enough to be pulled tight to avoid the pieces moving or sliding once assembled.

Drilled stitch holes

Rounding out stitch holes

Polishing stitch holes

Stitching materials together
Sewing acrylic

Finished stitching

PRECISION ENGINEERING

If a designer has access to precision cutting and machining equipment, then it is possible to incorporate complex fixings into the pieces. For example, a screw thread can be cut into or onto nylon, allowing parts to be screwed together, or precision slots used to assemble structures from interlocking pieces. Tapered rods can be slotted into holes and either pinned or held by their own friction.

Cutting a thread into nylon

heat fusion

Plastics can be heated until they soften sufficiently to fuse in their gel phase, however this may not be practical if the plastic has a high melting point, as it will require the plastic to be heated close to its melting point, making it difficult to handle safely.

Fragments of acrylic

However, acrylic has a relatively low melting point and, with care, it can be heated to slightly above 140°C, when the body of the material will become increasingly flexible (the gel phase) and the surface of the acrylic becomes 'tacky' as the surface energy that results in bonding increases.

Heating fragments with hot air gun

At 140°C+ the acrylic becomes gel-like

This allows two heated pieces of acylic to bond together without the need for an adhesive. The quality of the bond will depend on the type of acrylic used (extruded acrylic performs better than cast acrylic), the temperature of both pieces and the pressure applied to them. It is recommended that scrap material is used to conduct experiments to determine the desired results before use on final pieces.

Fragments assembled & pressed together

Pieces of acrylic from fine grains to large pieces can be used, as long as they are in the gel phase when pressed together. It is possible to create three-dimensional structures using this process, giving the appearance of an object created from fragments of glass etc.

Fused acrylic fragments

7 forming plastics

Heat-treated polypropylene flower jewellery

cold-forming plastics

TENSION-FORMING FLEXIBLE PLASTICS

The resilient and springy nature of some plastics makes them ideal materials for forming structural shapes by adding a curve. A curve in an even strip of these materials will be smooth and regular, and will give a pleasing visual line without any other forming. Sheets of 800 microns and above tend to be stiff enough to support these forms without additional support, and they will simply require a method of holding the form in place (see Designing catches and fittings, page 86). For finer sheets (500 microns or less) the edge may need to be wired.

WIRING THE EDGE

Although jewellery pieces made from flexible plastics can be formed by curving sheets and holding them under their own tension to give an aesthetic form, the finer the sheet the more delicate the structure and the more susceptible it becomes to distortion. With sheets of 500 microns or less, it can be beneficial to support the structure by applying a 0.8 mm hardened stainless steel wire to the edge of the piece.

Stainless steel wire offers a strong but formable edging wire that will not corrode and is sufficiently resilient to withstand normal handling of jewellery. Precious-metal wires do not offer the same resilience and their higher cost makes them less cost-effective.

Stainless steel wire can be pre-formed by winding it around a mandrel. Once released from the mandrel the wire will open up slightly, so use a smaller mandrel than the final size required.

Coiling wire around a mandrel

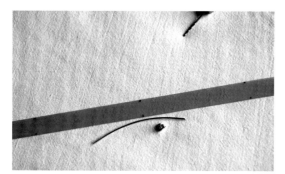

Materials: silver ball joint, 0.5 mm silver wire, plastic, stainless steel wire

Clip ball joint over stainless steel wire and edge of the plastic

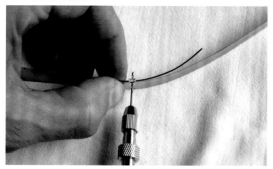

Drill through the plastic

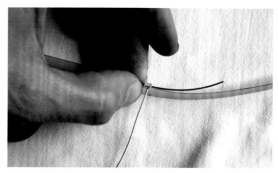

Insert silver wire

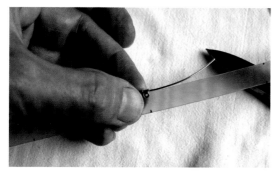

Cut silver wire

Press with parallel pliers to secure

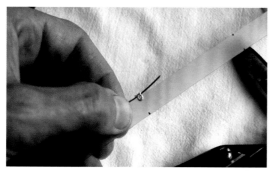

Ball joint ready for stainless steel wire
Fixing ball joints

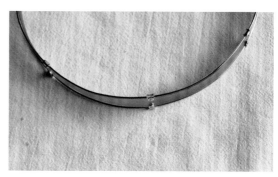

Finished wired edge

When the stainless wire has been formed to the correct size, it must be fitted to the edge of the piece of jewellery. A simple and effective method of doing this is to use the ball joints supplied by most jewellery findings suppliers. These clip over the wire and can be pressed onto the edge of the plastic. Once in place, a hole can be drilled through the ball joint hole and a silver wire inserted to fix the ball joint into place; in this way the wire can be securely fastened.

It is also necessary to secure the end of the wire. This is best done by ensuring that the end of the wire can be fed into the catch or fitting that secures the piece or finishes the end. NB It is essential to allow sufficient width inside the fitting for the wire and the plastic.

Wire inserted into fitting

CURLING

Long polymers give plastic its properties of resilience and flexibility; when subjected to force the material will flex and, as long as the force is not great enough to crease the material, it will spring back.

However, it is possible to create a permanent curve in the material by distorting the polymer structure sufficiently to stretch it without causing the material to discolour, break or crease. This is done in the same way as curling paper or ribbon, where the material is drawn over a curved former while under tension. This will cause the outside face to stretch while the inside edge remains unchanged. The result is a curve in the material that cannot be removed.

Care should be taken to avoid over-stressing the material; if the material is placed under sufficient stress the polymer will be damaged and this will appear as a milky or white mark in the body of the material (micro-cracking of the plastic).

Drawing material over a curved former

Permanent curl

Stressed polypropylene

PLASTIC MEMORY

The polymer structure and resilience of many flexible plastics produces an effect that can be described as 'plastic memory', and this is particularly true of polypropylene. If a piece of the material is stored lightly curled (not sufficient to damage the polymer structure), it will initially remain partly curled when it is removed from storage. However, if the material is allowed to warm gently, it will 'remember' its former shape and it will recover its original form. This is particularly useful if delicate jewellery has been stored poorly and becomes distorted: simply place the piece in a warm position and it should reshape itself.

Rigid plastics can be heated until they become pliable and then moulded. If they are then re-heated, they will exhibit a degree of plastic memory and recover some of their original shape.

Plastic memory will only be observed if the work has not been subjected to temperatures that are high enough to allow the polymer structure to flow; if this has occurred, the plastic will have been subject to thermoforming (see Thermoforming plastics, page 78) and the change in shape will be permanent.

NB

Delicate plastic jewellery can be damaged by exposure to direct heat from the sun through glass, high-temperature lamps, etc. and care should be taken when displaying and storing plastic jewellery. The temperature will depend on the glass transition and melting point of the plastic used – the lower these temperatures, the more sensitive the plastic is to heat.

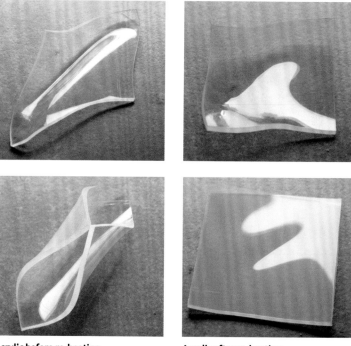

Acrylic before re-heating

Acrylic after re-heating

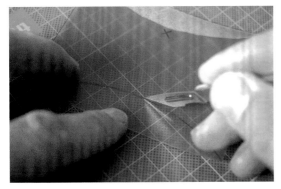

Scoring polypropylene with a scalpel

Folding along score line

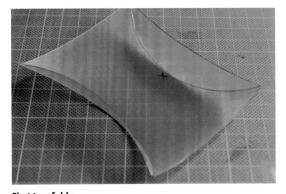

First two folds

Example of scoring and folding

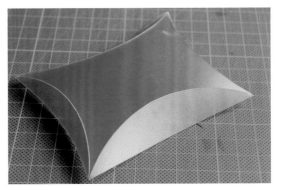

Second two folds

SCORING AND FOLDING

Flexible plastics can be scored and folded in much the same way as paper, allowing simple elements to be given a three-dimensional form.

For example, with polypropylene sheets of 280 microns it is possible to effectively score the surface by placing it on a soft surface and then tracing the required line with a blunt point. A constant and even pressure will produce an even, well-defined line that will readily fold.

On 500 micron sheet it is necessary to score the outside of the fold with a scalpel blade, taking care not to cut too deeply into the material. The fold can then be bent away from the cut to provide a neat and clean fold line. NB Scoring and folding may result in some damage to the polymer structure that appears as a white mark (micro-cracking) along the line of the fold.

As the thickness of the material increases it becomes more difficult to achieve a clean fold. The manufacturer's recommendation is to apply localised heat to the fold line and then fold using a former inside to ensure the correct shape is achieved.*

NB

*The description of this technique is based on the manufacturer's guidance and is not the result of direct experience.

thermoforming plastics

All of the plastics described in this work are thermoplastics, which means that they will soften and melt when heated, rather than thermoset plastics, which, once cured do not soften when heated.

This means that a thermoplastic can be heated until it softens sufficiently to be moulded, extruded or cast and then cooled to create a permanent three-dimensional form.

For example, polypropylene is a thermoplastic with a relatively low melting point, so it is possible to heat and manipulate it easily. At a temperature of 160°C the polymer melts and begins to flow, at which point it can be moulded and formed. This is the same process that is used to form all polypropylene products from sheets to bottles and buckets.

In most cases, polypropylene in its semi-liquid state is forced into a metal mould to form the shape; it is then cooled and ejected to allow the mould to be used repeatedly. These mould tools can be extremely complex and are therefore expensive to produce.

However, it is possible to apply some of these principles with very simple equipment. Heat can be applied either in a conventional oven, to heat a larger area of plastic, or in a more localised manner by using a hot-air gun.

USING AN OVEN

By simply heating a piece of sheet, the whole mass will become semi-liquid, which makes handling difficult. A practical solution to this is to mount the sheet into a metal frame – the frame will take longer to heat up and therefore the material trapped in it will remain cooler and less fluid. This means that the sheet can be removed from the oven with relative ease.

Care should be taken to control the temperature of the oven so that the material does not become too liquid and simply flow out of the frame. As most ovens are not accurate enough to set an exact temperature, it is necessary to conduct tests with each appliance to determine the best settings for the material used.

Once the sheet has been removed from the oven it can either be placed over a simple former or allowed to distort under its own weight while it cools, giving some basic 3D form to the sheet. With practice it is possible to produce a range of different effects that can then be used in the design of jewellery. Once the material has cooled, the polymer solidifies and can be handled as before.

Heating polypropylene in an oven

VACUUM-FORMING

A sheet of plastic heated in an oven can be applied to a simple vacuum-forming box. Once the plastic is placed over the box and the edge sealed, the vacuum will draw out the air and pull the molten plastic sheet down tightly over the form underneath.

This process gives a much more accurate result than simply placing a hot sheet of plastic over a simple former, and complex shapes may be achieved.

There are commercially available vacuum-forming machines, however it is possible to construct a simple vacuum-forming box. (See Appendix 1: Constructing a vacuum-former, page 128.)

Heating PP on a vacuum-former using an oven

Example of vacuum-forming over small shapes

Vacuum applied

Polypropylene fixed over ceramic former
Localised heating

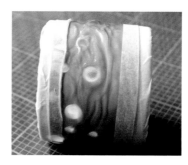

Heat from hot-air gun distorts the PP

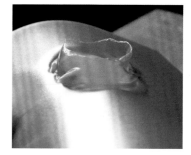

PP removed from former when cold

LOCALISED HEATING

It is possible to heat localised areas of a sheet of plastic using a hot-air gun. These are simple to use but you cannot adjust the temperature output of the gun, therefore the heat must be controlled by varying the distance of the gun from the sheet and the length of time that the heat is applied.

With practice it is possible to carefully control the temperature at a specific point and to use this to allow local manipulation of the sheets, rather than across the whole surface.

A simple application of this technique is to apply pressure to the molten part of the sheet and use this to stretch an area of the sheet. By using different forms it is possible to vary the resulting deformation.

Even when molten, most polymers have a high level of structural integrity and will continue to stretch until they form a very fine, delicate film, which is almost transparent. Having reached this point they cool and solidify rapidly, and further pressure will tear the film. These features may be used to create unusual effects within the material or design of a piece of jewellery, providing a more organic feel or variations in transparency.

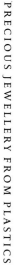

Heating polypropylene with a hot-air gun
Tears and transparency

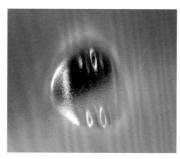

Localised melting in PP

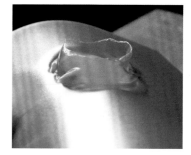

Hot air tears PP and thin areas
become transparent

thermoforming acrylic

As acrylic has a relatively narrow glass transition temperature, combined with a relatively low melting point and rigid nature, it makes an interesting material for experimentation with thermoforming. This characteristic of acrylic allows it to be moulded and formed in many different ways that can be used in the design and development of jewellery.

Rigid cold acrylic

When heated, acrylic deflects under its own weight

Softening and deflection

HEATING ACRYLIC

In order to ensure that the acrylic mass heats evenly, it is necessary to ensure that heat is applied relatively slowly, allowing it to be conducted through the body of the material before the surface is damaged by over-heating.

Strip heaters or hot-air guns are ideal methods for heating acrylic. Heat is generated through an electrical element and convection transfers the heat to the acrylic mass through the medium of passive or forced air flow. As the heat is created by resistance in the electrical element rather than combustion, no smoke, ash or carbon particles are produced that might contaminate the acrylic. (Heating acrylic with a direct flame can result in surface charring and discolouration and is therefore not recommended.)

As the temperature of the acrylic rises, the material will soften. This can be detected by pressing the surface gently with a heat-proof probe or by observing the deflection that occurs under the material's own weight.

Bubbling acrylic

BUBBLING

If the acrylic is heated sufficiently rapidly, volatile components in the body of the material will 'outgas', resulting in the formation of bubbles. This may or may not be a desired effect, depending on the design of the jewellery. However, the bubbling is irreversible and, if not required for the design being made, the material must be discarded and replacement materials should be heated slowly and with more care.

If bubbling is required, it is possible to control the size and number of bubbles by controlling the rate and duration of the heating. It is recommended that scrap material is used to conduct experiments to determine the desired results before use on final pieces.

STRETCHING ACRYLIC

Once acrylic has been heated to a gel, it is possible to stretch it before it cools. This will create an elongated and thinned section and, if stretched sufficiently, the mass will break, at which point it will have formed a long, fine filament.

The process must be conducted sufficiently quickly so that the mass of material does not cool and solidify, which is particularly likely when working with small pieces or when the material is stretched into fine elements.

Once cooled, fine filaments are also relatively delicate in nature and can easily be damaged or broken; this must be considered when designing the pieces.

PRESSURE LAMINATING

The gel form of acrylic can also be subjected to pressure by crushing it in a press. In this way it is possible to fuse two pieces of heated acrylic together to encapsulate thin materials between the layers.

A metal book press can be used effectively for this purpose, and it has the added advantage that the metal will help conduct away the heat from the crushed pieces once the press has been tightened, causing the acrylic to solidify in the crushed shape.

It is important to ensure that the encapsulated materials bond effectively to the acrylic or that sufficient contact between the sheets of acrylic is maintained, otherwise the resulting piece will delaminate when handled.

An example of this is seen when acetate film is encapsulated between acrylic pieces. The acrylic does not bond to the acetate and unless there is contact directly between the pieces of acrylic, the two parts separate easily once cooled.

Crushing acrylic in a book press

Once the technique of pressure laminating has been mastered, it is possible to encapsulate a wide range of fine materials between the pieces of acrylic. Materials that can be used include:

- wire
- thread
- glitter
- sequins
- fine foil and gold leaf
- open-weave textiles.

It is possible to experiment with many materials and the possibilities in terms of colour, texture and finish are almost limitless (see Precious plastic jewellery projects, page 119).

Pressure laminated acrylic with acetate film

Acrylic fails to bond to acetate

Examples of pressure laminating

Acetate can be peeled away

Acrylic with acetate removed
Acetate encapsulation and failure

RE-HEATING
PRESSURE-LAMINATED ACRYLIC

While working with material that had been pressure laminated, some pieces that did not appear to have been crushed sufficiently were re-heated. This revealed that the acrylic pieces exhibited a degree of shape 'memory'. Although fused to other materials, the acrylic tended to recover some of its original shape when heated back to the gel phase. The resulting pieces tended to distort and twist where the acrylic pulled back into shape and was resisted by the fused materials.

In some cases the resulting pieces were of interesting forms that could be used in the production of jewellery.

VACUUM-FORMING

Acrylic is frequently vacuum-formed in industrial processes, to produce simple three-dimensional shapes such as display stands and skylight domes. In the same way as polypropylene can be vacuum-formed, so can acrylic sheets. However, due to the thickness of the acrylic materials available, the time taken to heat acrylic is greater and corresponds to the thickness used.

With acrylic being far more rigid than polypropylene at room temperature, any pieces that are formed should account for the fact that as the material stretches in the forming process, it will become thinner and more delicate, once cooled.

Extruded and cast acrylic will perform differently when vacuum-formed and extruded acrylic is generally better for deeper shapes because of its lower density and resistance to shattering (see Appendix 1: Constructing a vacuum-former, page 128).

Material	Suitable for thermoforming
Polypropylene	Yes
Acrylic	Yes
Nylon 6,6	Yes
Polystyrene	Yes
PVC	Yes*
Polyethylene	Yes*

* Different formulations of these materials will alter their performance in thermoforming, and it is essential that materials are tested before use.

Before re-heating
Re-heating pressure-laminated acrylic

After re-heating

8 designing catches and fittings

When designing jewellery that uses sheet plastic, considerable thought is required to determine the best way in which to cover any joint in the material, for example a tubular bracelet of polypropylene cannot be cut from a sheet without creating a point at which the material must be joined in some way.

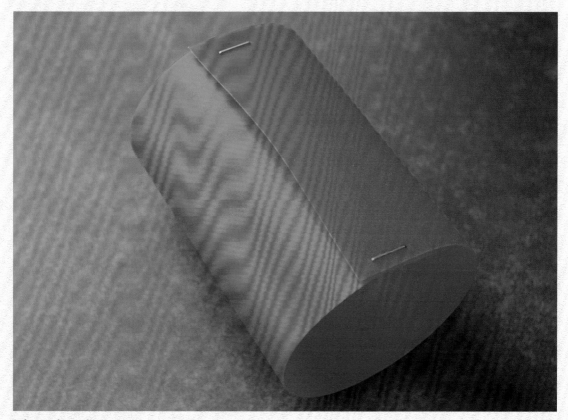

Polypropylene tube

In order to produce an aesthetically pleasing piece of jewellery, any joints or ends must be finished to a high standard. This is difficult to achieve by simply using an adhesive to bond items together. A solution that incorporates the use of precious metals will give the final piece a more jewellery-like quality and help the consumer to accept the final piece as something more than just plastic.

There are a wide range of different fittings that can be used to finish pieces effectively; a few examples are given below.

hollow fittings

This covers a wide range of potential fittings for covering joins and ends of sheet plastics. The fittings are constructed of thin silver sheets (0.7 mm) and are formed to create a hollow space that will slide over the sheet material.

The depth of the fitting can be tailored to accept one or more layers of the plastic, depending on the design requirements. In general, the following rule applies to the depth of the fitting:

No. of layers x thickness of the material + 0.5 mm

Therefore a fitting that will hold three layers of 500 micron (0.5 mm) polypropylene would be 2 mm deep. This allows sufficient space for the application of the adhesive but ensures that the profile of the fitting remains close to the surface of the sheets, creating a strong but effective finish.

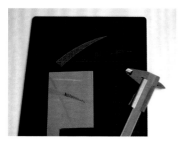

Materials: 0.7 mm silver and template for cap

Cutting silver strip

Straighten silver strip

Bend strip to fit template

Solder strip onto silver sheet

Check the fit of the template

Sand down strip until even

Solder on the second side

Clip off excess silver

File edges flat

Sand edges of fitting

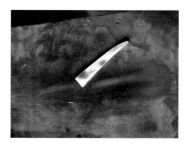

Sand sides of fitting and polish

Finished fitting in place

Making an end cap

END CAPS

This is the simplest form of hollow fitting and is designed to cover the end; in doing so it will also secure multiple layers together and provide some weight to the end of the piece, making it less likely to 'flap about'.

The outline of the cap can follow the same line as the plastic, creating a simple but effective finish that protects the end of the material while binding it into place.

The basic method of production is illustrated on the left.

For a fitting designed to cover two layers of 500 micron polypropylene sheet, cut a strip of 0.7 mm silver that is 1.5 mm wide and long enough to go around the sides of the fitting. Ensure the strip is straight and then carefully bend it to fit the profile of the cap. Once the profile is correct, carefully lay it onto a piece of 0.7 mm silver sheet and solder it down one side, taking care that the shape does not distort while it is heating.

Once cooled, clip away the excess silver sheet and sand down the other face of the profile strip to ensure it is flat and parallel to the first sheet. Turn the fitting over and place onto a second sheet of 0.7 mm silver and solder up the joint – for fittings with a wide 'mouth' the silver sheet will tend to sag under the heat, this can distort the fitting and make it hard to polish. This can be combated by placing a small wedge of steel of the correct thickness in the mouth to support the silver while it is soldered.

Clip away the excess silver sheet, then carefully file the edges of the fitting until they are flat and even, taking care not to file through the silver.

Polish the fitting carefully; for the best results hand-polishing gives a finer edge and greater clarity of design. Make sure the fitting is clean and dry inside before applying the adhesive to the polypropylene and inserting it into the fitting.

Materials for hand polishing Sanding sticks (180–1200 grit) and leather buff stick and polish.

CAPS WITH CHAINS

For fittings that are designed to form part of a closure, for example on a collar, the caps can be constructed with hooks and chains so that they have a degree of adjustment. These work well with polypropylene as the material's natural springiness provides the tension to hold the hook in place.

For a fitting designed to cover three layers of 500 micron polypropylene sheet, take a piece of 0.7 mm silver which is twice the length of the fitting, plus the depth of the fitting and as wide as the width of the polypropylene. Carefully score the middle of the sheet with two parallel lines that are 2 mm apart (3 x 500 microns + 0.5 mm) and then fold the sheet over a 2 mm-thick piece of flat metal, to create a deep U-shaped channel. Carefully sand down one side to ensure that the edges are parallel and then solder this to a sheet of 0.7 mm silver. Once cooled, remove the excess silver and repeat the process for the other side of the fitting. For fittings with a wide 'mouth' the silver sheet will tend to sag under the heat, which can distort the fitting and make it hard to polish. This can be combated by placing a small wedge of steel of the correct thickness in the mouth to support the silver while it is soldered.

The edges of the fitting can then be carefully filed down until level with the sides and the end. Sand down the end of the cap with 1000 grit paper until a fine finish is achieved. Take a silver jump link and cut into two equal parts. Stand the cap on its open edge and heat carefully until the jump link can be soldered into position. (Easy silver solder paste is best used for this fine work.)

The fitting can then be carefully sanded and polished. Once completed, a small hook can be fabricated and soldered onto a length of chain, this can then be soldered onto the fitting with a jump link – taking care to avoid heating the fitting and spoiling the polish. The cap is then ready for fitting onto the piece.

Making the cap and adding the link, hook and chain

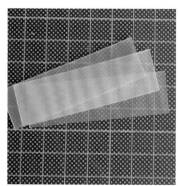

Three layers of 500 micron polypropylene

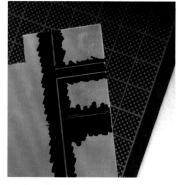

Mark out fitting

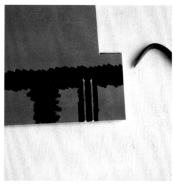

Score fold lines

Fold silver sheet into U shape

Solder ends into place

Check fit on polypropylene

File down edges

Sand down fitting to fine finish

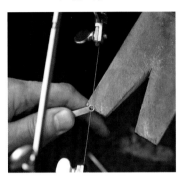

Cut silver jump link in half

Solder one half of jump link to fitting

Bend hook out of silver wire

Solder hook onto chain

Solder chain onto fitting with jump link

Give fittings a final polish

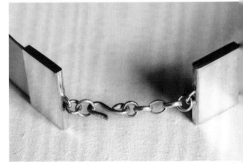

Pair of fittings in place

TUBULAR FITTINGS

When two ends of plastic are to be joined, two factors must be considered. First, the joint will affect the curvature of the piece – if the ends are overlapped then this part will be thicker and stiffer. The second factor is that transparent plastics will show where the adhesive has been applied and this will not add to the aesthetic of the piece. A simple solution is to produce a tubular fitting to cover the join and to maintain the curvature.

For a fitting designed to cover two layers of 500 micron polypropylene sheet, cut a strip of 0.7 mm silver that is 1.5 mm wide and long enough to go along both sides of the fitting with approximately 10 mm extra for each side. Cut this into two equal halves. Bend 10 mm of each strip at 90° to the rest of the strip.

Take a piece of 0.7 mm silver that is slightly longer than the length of the fitting, and a few millimetres wider. Place one of the strips on the edge of the sheet and solder into place. (The 90° angle will support the strip while you do this.) Take the other strip and solder into place along the other edge, allowing sufficient space for the polypropylene.

Clip off the excess sheet and carefully sand the top edges of both strips to ensure that they are level and even. Carefully bend the strip over a mandrel to match the curve of the piece being made.

Curve a second sheet to match the fitting and solder into place, ensuring that both sides are fully bonded. Clip away the excess silver sheet, then carefully file the edges of the fitting until they are flat and even, taking care not to file through the silver.

Polish the fitting carefully; for the best results hand-polishing gives a finer edge and greater clarity of design. Make sure the fitting is clean and dry inside before applying the adhesive to the polypropylene and inserting it into the fitting.

Materials: two strips of 0.7 mm silver and silver sheet

Solder a silver strip down one edge

Repeat along the second edge

Curve the fitting over a mandrel

Curve second silver sheet to match

Solder second silver sheet into place

Remove excess silver

Making a tubular fitting

Sand and polish fitting

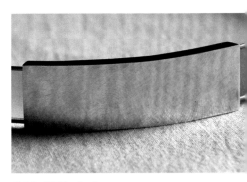

Finished fitting in place

Applying a tubular fitting with hot melt

CHAINS AND HOOKS

To fasten two pieces of flexible plastic together along part of their length it is possible to use a small fitting that uses a chain with a hook or clasp, secured to the surface of the sheet.

Using 0.7 mm silver sheet, punch out two small discs of silver. Solder on a length of threaded silver wire (see Screw fittings, page 60) to one side and half a jump link to the other side and carefully polish the fitting. Once completed, a small hook can be fabricated and soldered onto a length of chain; this can then be soldered onto the fitting with a jump link – taking care to avoid heating the fitting and spoiling the polish. The second disc can be treated in the same way but the chain will not require a hook, just a plain jump link.

Pierce a hole in each of the pieces of plastic sheet and insert the screw threads and attach a threaded ball.

Materials: silver wire, silver chain, silver sheet, jump links and threaded balls

Solder threaded silver and half a jump link to the silver disc

Solder the hook and chain onto the fitting using a jump link

Pierce a hole in the plastic and insert thread, then attach threaded ball

Finished fitting in place

SLIDE PLATES

When a design requires a simple, low-profile fitting, particularly when stitching flexible plastics, a slide plate can be used.

The plate works on the 'keyhole' slot principle, using the natural tension of the plastic to keep the fitting secure while the piece is being worn.

Use silver sheet that is stiff enough to withstand the stress of the design without bending or warping (minimum 0.7 mm) and cut this to the width of the required fitting. Mark out and drill two holes, large enough to accept a threaded ball (see Screw fittings, page 60). Then cut two short channels away from the holes in the opposite direction to the plastic it will be attached to.

Drill fine holes along the line of the stitching used on the piece and sew the fitting onto the sheet. On the other side of the part to be joined, add two screw fittings with sufficient thread to allow the silver plate to slide under the balls, once they have passed through the holes.

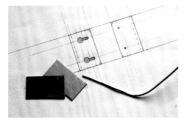

Materials: silver sheet, silver wire and threaded balls

Cut plates and mark out keyhole

Drill out and cut keyhole slots

Solder length of threaded wire to second plate and attach threaded balls

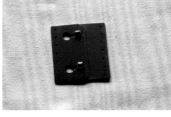

Polish both halves of fitting

Drill out stitch holes in silver fittings, mark these onto plastic and pierce

Stitch fitting onto plastic with fine, strong thread

Finished fitting in place

Making and fitting a slide plate

Materials: silver tube, silver sheet, gemstone and silver bar

Cut two sections of silver tube, the inner longer than the outer

Solder onto silver sheet

CHANNEL FITTINGS

In designs where a number of fine plastic parts are to be inserted, a U-shaped channel can be formed and the ends of the elements can then be glued in. A good example of this is a circular channel formed around a setting.

For a channel that will accept three rows of 500 micron polypropylene, take the required setting and measure the diameter, then take this measurement and add 4 mm (3 x 500 microns + 0.5 mm per side x 2 sides = 4 mm) and select a tube with this internal diameter.

Cut a section of the tube that is just shorter than the height of the setting – this allows the stone to be set without the channel obstructing the setting process. Ensure that the tube is cut at 90°. Take the setting and solder onto a piece of sheet (minimum 0.7 mm), then carefully place the piece of tube over the setting so that it is evenly spaced all round and solder into place.

Clip away the excess silver sheet and carefully file the edges of the fitting until they are flat and even, taking care not to file through the silver. The complete setting can then be mounted onto a ring shank, or onto a threaded bar as illustrated.

Polish the fitting carefully (for the best results hand-polishing gives a finer edge and greater clarity of design), then set the stone. Make sure the fitting is clean and dry inside before applying the adhesive to the polypropylene pieces and inserting them into the fitting. For fine pieces, it may be necessary to hold them in place for a few seconds while the adhesive sets.

Insert collar to support stone & solder in

Trim sheet, file and sand smooth

Solder on threaded bar & make back plate

Set stone and polish
Making a channel fitting

Finished channel fitting

Cut polypropylene star

Pierce centre of star and insert threaded fitting

Apply adhesive to ends of star and glue into channel

First set of frills in place

Cut individual frills and glue into channel

Apply beads and attach (see Attaching beading, page 64)

Cut second polypropylene star, apply beads and add to setting

Adding polypropylene to a channel fitting

Finished channel fitting

Materials: silver frame (in this case a ring) with post soldered on and silver tube

Insert post into hole in plastic

Add the silver tube

Rivet over the end of the silver post
Making a pinned fitting and adding polypropylene

PINNED FITTINGS

To apply an element to a silver framework, where the use of screw fittings may be too obtrusive, it is possible to create a hybrid fitting that is part way between a screw fitting and a rivet.

Once the silver frame has been constructed, carefully drill out 1.5 mm holes where the material should be attached. Then take a length of 1.5 mm wire that will fit through the hole and leave a post that is long enough to pass through the plastic, plus approximately 2 mm. Solder the wire into place, then clean and polish the frame.

Make a small hole in the plastic pieces and slide them onto the post. Take a fine piece of silver tube with an internal diameter of 1.5 mm and cut a length of 1 mm. This small length of tube will act as a washer and should be added to the post, leaving approximately 0.75 mm of the post exposed. Carefully support the frame and rivet over the end post to hold the piece of tube in place.

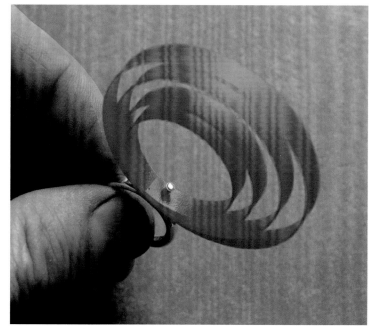

Finished pinned fitting

INVISIBLE HOOK FITTINGS

This type of fitting was specifically developed for joining plastic strips without any visible closure, and is therefore useful for pieces where the highest possible aesthetic finish is demanded.

Constructing these fittings is a high-precision process that requires tolerances of only a fraction of a millimetre. This means that these fittings are time consuming to produce and therefore add significantly to the cost of the piece of jewellery. In addition to this, it is not obvious how the fittings open and therefore it is critical to ensure that customers understand how to operate the catch, otherwise they may damage the fitting by forcing it apart or twisting it.

It is important to ensure that the two halves of the fitting are completely symmetrical and that the plates are truly square when finished (i.e. that the angles are 90°), otherwise the fitting will appear crooked, even if the difference is only a fraction of a millimetre.

First, calculate the size of the plate required, the internal slot must be sufficient to accept the required number of layers of plastic, plus a small allowance for fitting and adhesive, and wide enough for the width of the strips of plastic, plus any wires used along the edge (see Wiring the edge, page 73).

For example, a design uses three layers of 800 micron plastic that is 12 mm wide and will be wired on both edges with 800 micron wire. The slot must be 3 x 800 microns + 200 microns for the first layer + 100 microns each for each additional layer = 2800 microns (2.8 mm) deep. The slot must be 12 mm + 2 x 800 microns wide (800 microns per wire) + 200 microns per wire = 14 mm.

Invisible hook fitting - cut-away view

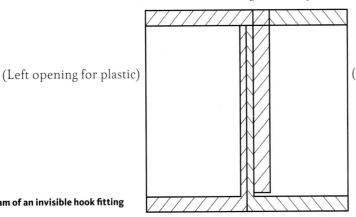

(Left opening for plastic)   (Right opening for plastic)

Diagram of an invisible hook fitting

Materials: silver sheet, cut to size and shape

Solder edges and hook to plates

Sand face of plates to ensure they are flat and even

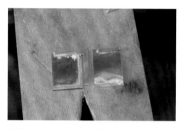

Solder the second plate into place and check fit

Plate without hook has an open side that must be covered

The final dimension, the length of the fitting, can be varied depending on the design requirements, but it should be a minimum of 10 mm per side to allow sufficient adhesive application inside the fitting.

Using the dimensions above as an example, the fitting is constructed as follows:

Cut a plate of silver sheet (minimum thickness 0.7 mm) that is 18 mm wide by 25 mm long, ensure that the plate is cut and filed to 90° at all corners and that the edges are straight. The plate is then cut in two to give two pieces of 18 x 12 mm. Along one of the 12 mm edges, on each plate, solder a 2 mm-wide strip of silver that is 3 mm thick. On one plate solder a 2 mm wide L-shaped piece of 2 x 3 mm silver that is 15 mm along both arms of the 'L'; this is soldered along the top edge of the silver sheet, with one arm of the 'L' overhanging the edge of the sheet by 1 mm (see photos). Solder a 1 x 3 mm silver strip along the edge of this plate, parallel to the overhanging arm of the L to complete the three sides of the fitting, leaving the fourth side free.

On the second plate, solder a 2 x 10 mm strip of 3 mm silver along the other edge of the plate, leaving a 2 mm gap at one end; this will leave a gap for the hook to slot into this side of the fitting. Solder a 2 x 10 mm strip of 3 mm all along the opposite edge.

Cut two plates slightly larger than 18 x 12 mm and solder these onto the fittings to form the second face of the fitting, leaving a hollow that is 3 x 14 mm approximately inside the fitting. Carefully file away excess silver from the plates and ensure that the angles of 90° are maintained.

On the plate without the 'hook', the fitting is not yet complete and it is necessary to solder a 1 mm-thick facing plate onto the end with the gap for the hook to slot into the fitting. Solder this into place and file away the excess silver. Carefully slide a piercing saw through the fitting and out of the slot for the hook and cut down the facing plate to a depth of 2 mm and 3 mm in width. This allows the hook to slide into place completely. Carefully clean and file both plates and slide the hook into the slot of the second half of the fitting, trimming the length to allow the hook to slide in completely.

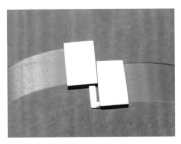

Once assembled, the plates should fit closely together, with a smooth, straight joint. Measure the two plates and trim the length to ensure that they are perfectly matched. Carefully sand and polish the two plates until they are completely even and smooth on all sides when assembled.

The finished result should look like two rectangular plates that appear to be held together without any visible sight of attachment, except where the hook on one plate sides into the side of the other plate.

When inserting the plastic and wire into the fitting, ensure that they do not obstruct the hook from being inserted into the plate; to do this it is best to glue the plastic into place with the fitting assembled, however, do not allow the adhesive to bond the hook into the fitting!

Solder on silver strip

Trim edges, sand plates

The fitting in action

Invisible hook fitting in position awaiting final polish

9 dyeing plastics

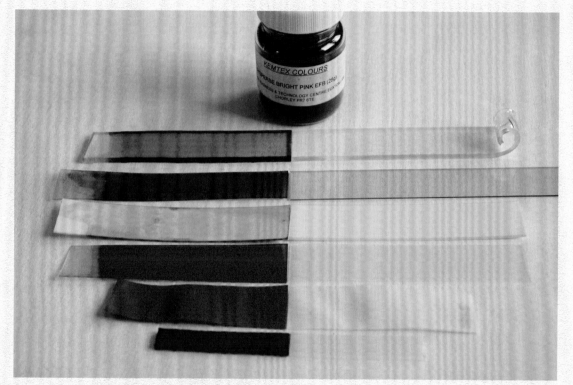

Dye samples on different plastics Left: dye samples with Disperse Bright Pink EFB. Right: undyed samples. From top to bottom: acrylic, PVC, Polystyrene, Polypropylene, Polyethylene (HDPE), Nylon 6

When first researching the properties of polypropylene a number of manufacturers were approached and asked for technical details about the material and about the possibility of producing customised colours of sheet material. In general the answer was that it was possible to produce polypropylene sheet in almost any colour but with a minimum order quantity of 2 tonnes, because the basic polymer is batch coloured post-polymerisation. In most applications 2 tonnes of material is a significant investment, but within the context of jewellery manufacture, this could represent a lifetime's production of work from just one colour. (However, polypropylene is available is a wide range of colours and the main manufacturers continually compete to produce new variations to meet the changing trends in the retail market.)

When this limitation became apparent, the manufacturers were asked if it was possible to alter the colour of the sheets post-production, without exception they indicated that this was not possible.

This is typical of all plastics: it is possible to manufacture a wide range of colours and shades, however the scale of production makes this prohibitive for the jewellery designer.

off-the-shelf colours

Many manufacturers produce a range of colours, particularly for materials that are used for designer products and consumer markets. However, materials like Nylon 6,6 are principally used in industrial applications where a range of colours is not required. Therefore, it is frequently the case that suppliers may only carry a range limited to black, white and natural translucent sheets or a minimal range of the off-the-shelf colours.

So, in order to ensure that the widest possible range of colours was available to the designer, it was necessary to consider the possibility of dyeing plastic post-production. The dye type and performance will depend on the material being dyed.

the basic concept

The basic concept is to allow the dye to penetrate the plastic as much as possible. Under normal conditions (room temperature) most dyes have little effect on the materials. However, if the dye is used in combination with heat, the heat causes the molecular structure of the polymer to expand and to 'open up' sufficiently to let the very fine dye particles penetrate the dense structure of the plastic. When the plastic cools, the structure of the polymer closes and the dye particles are trapped in the structure permanently.

The key is to heat the plastic sufficiently, in the dye solution, to allow the dye to penetrate, but not to so high a temperature as to cause permanent damage to the plastic.

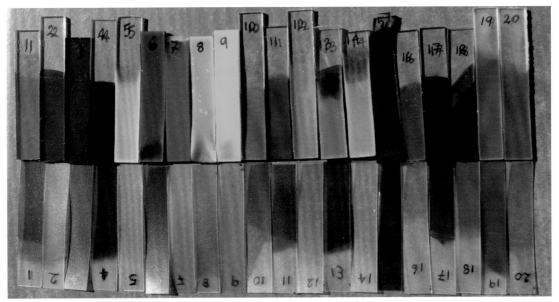

Disperse dye test samples Top row: acrylic. Bottom row: polypropylene.
Colours: 1 Disperse Bright Blue BG, 2 Disperse Scarlet Red EB, 3 Disperse Bottle Green 2B, 4 Disperse Navy Mixture, 5 Disperse Mid Yellow EG, 6 Disperse Lincoln Green EGB, 7 Disperse Fuchsia Red EXB, 8 Disperse Emerald Green G, 9 Disperse Aqua Turquoise GFS, 10 Disperse Bright Pink EFB, 11 Disperse Royal Blue EBN, 12 Disperse Lime Green 2G, 13 Disperse Turquoise Blue 7GN, 14 Disperse Bright Orange E2R, 15 Disperse Full Black EBT, 16 Disperse Golden Yellow R, 17 Disperse Claret Red EBD, 18 Disperse Rust Brown ER, 19 Disperse Mid Red EFG, 20 Disperse Vivid Violet E4R

POLYPROPYLENE

Despite the manufacturer's assertions that polypropylene cannot be dyed, and following consultation with a specialist dye supplier who had experience in dyeing acrylic, a sample of a disperse dye was tested to see if it would alter the colour of the polypropylene.

At room temperature the disperse dye had no effect on the polypropylene and once removed and washed the test sample was unchanged. However, understanding that the structure of polypropylene alters under the application of heat, the test was repeated at a temperature of approximately 80°C and after a period of approximately 30 minutes the sample was washed and examined: the result was a significant change in colour.

Further experimentation with an increased concentration of dye and a longer immersion time improved the colour penetration and, although not as strong as with other plastics (e.g. nylon), the results were effective enough to make the material useful in jewellery design.

However, care must be taken not to overheat the polypropylene as this would cause permanent distortion in the polymer structure.

ACRYLICS

There are some acrylic colours that cannot be dyed due to the availability of dye pigments – particularly in the case of fluorescent finishes. However there is a wide range of 'off-the-shelf' dyes that can be used to create a range of colours. Two types of dye are recommended for dyeing acrylics, these are:

- basic dyes
- disperse dyes.

NYLON 6,6

One potential limitation of nylon is the lack of off-the-shelf colours, in most cases nylon is produced in natural, white or black. Therefore it is necessary to dye the nylon in order to achieve a range of colours. Nylon 6,6 is more difficult to dye than other forms, due to its density and structure, however once the dyeing has been achieved it will be stable and resistant to fading.

Disperse dyes work effectively on nylon and tend to produce stronger colours compared to the same dye used on polypropylene.

POLYSTYRENE

Dyeing with a basic dye resulted in minimal dye absorption and poor colouration. However, the use of a disperse dye resulted in a moderate level of dye absorption and a fair level of colouration, although the dye absorption was not completely even across the tested samples. This may be the result of differences in the polystyrene material itself, therefore purchased materials should be tested thoroughly before use.

PVC

Dyeing PVC with a basic dye resulted in some dye absorption, but the resulting colours differed from the dye colour intended. (A blue dye resulted in a reddish colour and a red dye produced a brown colour.) In addition, the heat of the dye bath caused the PVC strip to distort, with the result that the dyed sample would have been difficult to use in some designs.

PVC dyes well with disperse dyes, producing a strong colour that is close to the original dye. However, exposure to heat resulted in the transparent samples becoming opaque and although this did not affect the dye absorption, it resulted in material remaining opaque rather than translucent. This fact should be considered if a transparent material is required for a design.

POLYETHYLENE

Dyeing with a basic dye resulted in minimal dye absorption and poor colouration.

Disperse dyes showed a fair level of absorption on the HDPE samples used, with a lighter but even finish to the dyed area.

As polyethylene is available in numerous forms it is not possible to give a comprehensive review of dyeing the material, however it is recommended that samples of polyethylene should be tested to determine the effect of disperse dyes on the material used.

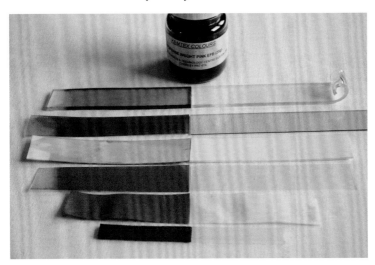

Example of dye absorption by different plastics Right: un-dyed samples. Left: dyed samples. Top to bottom: acrylic, PVC, polystyrene, polypropylene, HDPE, Nylon 6.

using disperse dyes

DYEING PROCESS

Disperse dyes can be purchased from the supplier below in small quantities. Thoroughly dissolve the desired amount of dye powder in boiling water, let the mixture cool to room temperature and stir well again. Prepare the dye bath by adding warm (38°–41°C) water into a non-reactive, stainless steel or enamel pot, then add the dissolved dye and stir well. Add the plastic pieces to be dyed, then slowly heat the dye bath (80°–95°C), stirring occasionally. Periodically check the material to assess the colour penetration. (If necessary add further dissolved dye.)

When the material has dyed sufficiently dyed, remove it from the dye bath and rinse under cold water.

An effective, simple dye bath is a conventional slow cooker. These are readily available, easy to use and relatively inexpensive. (However, it is recommended that this should not be used for food use after it has been used as a dye bath.)

If small elements are to be dyed, it is possible to place a glass, ceramic, stainless steel or even plastic container, filled with dye, in a slow cooker that is half filled with water. This will transfer the heat to the smaller dye baths and allow for more than one colour to be used at a time.

Examples of disperse dyes

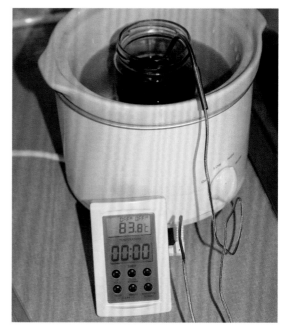

Set-up for plastic dyeing

using basic dyes

Historically, basic dyes presented health hazards, but recent developments in these dyes have led to the development of new formulations that are less hazardous and represent no greater risk than other dyes. When used on acrylics, they offer a high degree of colour-fastness, bright colours and darker shades than disperse dyes.

Examples of basic dyes

HEALTH AND SAFETY

Although dyes have been developed to reduce the hazards of handling and use, it is vital that anyone intending to use dyes should obtain the manufacturer's Safety Data Sheets to ensure that they understand and obviate the risks of use. The hazards will vary depending on the type and colour of the dye, as each one is based on different chemical constituents.

HEALTH AND SAFETY

It is good practice to wear protective gloves and a suitable breathing mask and eye protection to prevent accidental contact with the dye powders and solutions.

Dyes should be stored and used in areas that are not used for food, and they should not be allowed to contaminate areas where accidental skin/eye contact could occur.

In addition to this, care should be taken in the disposal of the residual dye material – if in doubt about how to dispose of any remaining solution, it is advisable to contact your local authority for advice.

Basic dyes work sufficiently well at 80–90°C but care should be taken to control the temperature and agitation of the dye solution to promote good 'levelling' (even penetration) of the dye. Dyeing may also be aided by the acidification of the dye solution with acetic acid or Glauber's salt (sodium sulphate). There are additives and auxiliary products that can be used to enhance the dyeing process, but these tend to be more hazardous and are therefore not recommended for small-scale dyeing.

DYE PENETRATION

Although the dyes penetrate and become permanent within the plastics, the dye does not penetrate deep into the surface of thick material but effectively dyes an outer layer only; this is only revealed once the material is cut or filed. Therefore, it is necessary to cut, file and shape elements *before* they are dyed, unless the design includes exposing areas of undyed plastic.

The degree of dye penetration will depend on the thickness of the material, the temperature of the dye bath and the length of time in the dye solution. However, the penetration is generally superficial and although this does not show unless the material is cut, it must be considered when handling dyed plastic.

Dyed acrylic block

Dyed block with front and back sanded and polished to show dye penetration

As the application of ethylene meth-acrylic acid dissolves the surface of the acrylic, it will also dissolve the dyed layer on the surface and this may result in variations in surface dye dispersion, leaving a pattern of streaks.

DIFFERENTIAL DYEING

Once the dyeing process has been mastered, it is possible to dye plastic elements differentially, for example, a strip of polypropylene treated with two dyes to create a multicoloured design in a material that is normally monochrome.

Examples of three different differential dyeing patterns are given below, in each case the original strip was a natural translucent material in 500 microns.

BI-COLOURED STRIPS

A strip is half immersed in the first dye bath and allowed to dye. It is then removed, washed and the other end is immersed in a second dye colour to create a two-coloured strip.

TRI-COLOURED STRIPS

The strip is first completely immersed in the base colour and allowed to dye. It is then removed, washed and one end dyed in a second colour. The strip is then removed, washed and the second end dyed. The result is a strip with the centre in the base colour and the ends in a colour that combines both the base colour and the second or third dye used.

GRADUATED STRIPS

If a strip is required to gradually fade from one colour to another, e.g. from yellow to red, the strip should first be completely dyed in the paler shade and then progressively dyed with darker shades, with less and less of the strip immersed each time, this will result in a graduated change in the shade.

FADING AND COLOUR FASTNESS

During the initial research phase a number of proprietary dyes (e.g. LaRiche Directions hair dyes) were tested on the material. Initial results showed some degree of success, depending on the make of dye. However, when the pieces were stored in natural light the dyes suffered from significant UV degradation and the colours gradually faded from the pieces; in some cases the dye disappeared completely.

Most dyes will degrade when exposed to UV light, however the stability of disperse dyes is greater than other materials trialled and no significant degradation was observed after several months of exposure to natural daylight.

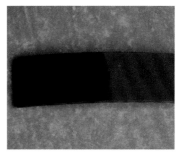

Example of a bi-coloured strip

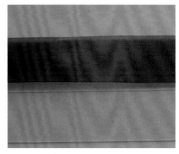

Example of a tri-coloured strip

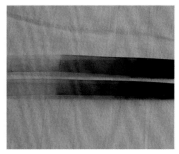

Example of a graduated strip

NB

It is recommended that all dyed materials are tested to ensure that their UV stability is appropriate to the jewellery application.

10 other decorative finishes

printing

It is possible to print on polypropylene and other plastics using either screen-printing or UV litho-printing. However, the type of ink used may impact on the results, for example some inks that have a high mineral oil distillate, which can cause distortion or curling of polypropylene sheets; vegetable/soya-based inks or similar can reduce the distortion.

NB

The processes described above are based on the manufacturer's guidance. The process described is not the result of direct experience and it is suggested that anyone wishing to pursue this process should contact the plastic and ink manufacturers for further advice.

HOT-FOIL BLOCKING

According to some of the plastics manufacturer's technical data, it is possible to apply a metallic foil design using a hot-foil blocking process with either a brass or steel block.

finishing and polishing rigid plastics

FILING AND SANDING

As acrylic is a relatively rigid plastic, it can be filed and shaped in the same way as wood or metal. As well as working by hand, it is practical to use machinery to remove the bulk of material and speed up the shaping process.

Care should be taken to ensure that the sanding equipment does not generate too much heat from friction, as this will result in clogging of the belt, build-up of plastic residue at the edge of the piece and possible melting of the piece being worked on. Suitable equipment includes:

- belt sander or linisher
- disc sander
- angle grinder with sanding pad
- power file.

Mini disc sander

BELT SANDER OR LINISHER

These tools are ideal for removing large areas of material and creating a flat surface; they are not effective for fine details or complex curves.

DISC SANDER

A vertical disc sander is effective at removing material from convex curves, particularly on the edges and ends of a piece of work.

Sanding an acrylic rod with a grinder

ANGLE GRINDER WITH SANDING PAD

Although an angle grinder must be held in one or both hands, it is possible to use the edge of the disc to carve forms into a block of acrylic. With practice, basic forms can be roughed out in large pieces of material and then refined by hand or with a power file to create complex curves.

POWER FILE

These tools offer a range of surfaces from a tight curve to a flexible face that can be used to shape pieces or remove finer amounts of material.

Sanding with a power file

Those intending to work with rigid plastics, such as acrylic, on a regular basis should consider the value of investing in all of these tools if they intend to make larger pieces of work.

GRADES OF SANDING BELTS AND DISCS

Sanding belts and discs are graded according to the size of the mesh through which particles can pass. The number, e.g. 80 grit, represents the number of openings in a linear inch (2.5 cm) – in this case 80 and therefore, the higher the number, the finer the particle size.

A low-number grit sanding belt will be coarser and will remove larger pieces of material and will consequently remove a given amount of material faster than a finer grit at the same speed and pressure.

However, this will also produce a coarser finish, leaving deeper scratches in the surface once the sanding is completed. To create a smooth, polished surface it is necessary to progressively increase the grade of the sanding belt, allowing each one to remove the scratches from the previous grade, until the surface is smooth enough to polish (approximately 800–1000 grit).

Sanding belts are not generally available at fine grades and it may be necessary for the final sanding stages to be done by hand.

FINISHING AND POLISHING

The principles of polishing rigid plastics like acrylic are similar to those of metals like silver and gold. Since acrylic is relatively soft, it is possible to take a shaped piece and sand the surface by hand. Using successively finer grades of wet and dry (silicon carbide) paper, the scratches can be gradually removed until the surface is even and can be given a final sanding with 1000-grade paper.

The surface can then be machine-buffed using a soft cotton mop and a suitable polishing compound, for example Vonax, produced by Canning-Lippert (Lippert-Unipol).

Care should be taken to avoid applying pressure to the acrylic with the mop during polishing, as the heat generated by the friction will result in the acrylic surface softening and the mop will then drag the softened material, creating a scar in the surface. The piece should be held firmly but the polish-laden mop should be allowed to brush gently over the surface to achieve the best results.

FLAME POLISHING

It is also possible to polish the edges of acrylic by applying a flame directly to the surface. This will result in the edges effectively melting slightly and the result is a highly glazed appearance that looks much like a polished surface. It is essential to apply only the minimum required heat, as overheating the edge will damage the piece.

Buffing acrylic on a polishing mop

design and aesthetics

There are many jewellery publications that deal with design, and good design is frequently seen through the lens of taste and fashion, which change over time. However, some factors remain constant, regardless of changing fashion.

functionality

Jewellery that cannot be worn, falls off or breaks too easily is unlikely to be successful and in general any piece of jewellery should be 'fit for purpose'. This is not an absolute as there are examples of conceptual jewellery that are unwearable, but these items may not fit the general description of jewellery being 'an item of personal adornment that is worn by a person'.

quality of finish

Art jewellery aims to demonstrate value through excellence in design, form and function. If the work attempts to meet these aspirations but is poorly constructed and badly finished, then these factors will undermine the aesthetic value that the design seeks to achieve.

design strategy

If you have mastered the techniques for working with a material, you are free to create whatever you wish – within the physical limitations of the material itself. Therefore, the design strategy should be the first point to consider when you sit down to develop your designs.

A design strategy considers the fundamental direction in which the work will go and the driving forces behind that direction. This, in turn, will impact on the sales of the work. Questions that you should ask yourself are:

▶ Why am I making this work?
▶ What do I want to achieve?
▶ Who is my audience?
▶ What do they want?

The answers to these questions will influence the direction your design will take. See the examples opposite.

ART JEWELLERY

A designer wishes to make work that proves their talent as an artist; they wish to receive recognition as a talented and outstanding artist in the eyes of those who collect and review the contemporary jewellery market. In this case the financial rewards may be secondary to the artistic achievement and the artist may hope that sales will follow artistic recognition. The work will be highly individual, ground-breaking and time-consuming to produce, and therefore expensive.

The result could be that the designer will receive high levels of recognition and lead the market in design and innovation, however the financial rewards may be limited by the cost of the work and the limited number of people who will wear such avant-garde work.

DESIGNER JEWELLERY

The individual may wish to create a body of work that will provide sufficient income for them to live on, in which case their work must appeal to a wide audience and suit the tastes and needs of the potential customers, for example it must be easy to wear but sufficiently unusual and attractive to stand out from the rest of the jewellery on display. Its price should be high enough to reflect the work that went into making it, but not so high that the majority of people cannot afford it.

The designer would then be in a position to produce and sell work on a regular basis, creating a wide distribution across their chosen market and receiving a relatively steady return.

PRODUCTION JEWELLERY

This work aims to create pieces that are attractive and available to the widest possible audience, with low production costs and lower prices. It is difficult for the individual maker to compete in this market, as they lack the investment to use mass-production processes, however it represents the opposite extreme to the art jewellery market.

The design strategy is really a simplified approach to the process that every product development group in every major corporation undertakes before investing their time and energy in developing a new product or service.

Once you have decided in which direction you wish to develop your work, you can consider the features that need to be incorporated into the design. These could include:
- How to make the work unique
- How easy the work is to wear
- How to reduce the production time.

making plastic jewellery precious

Beauty, creativity, uniqueness and quality are all features that do not relate to the material from which an item is made – if plastic jewellery incorporates these features, it will have a value in its own right.

However, there may still be some resistance to the fact that it has no intrinsic value. Some people may resist paying the price for designer jewellery if it is 'just plastic'. One solution to this resistance is to combine the plastics with traditional jewellery materials, such as silver and semi-precious stones. The cost of these is not prohibitive, but the work will be attributed a higher value because of the association with these traditional materials. In this way it is possible to enhance the appeal of the work to the widest possible audience, creating work that is innovative, high quality, unique and has some associated intrinsic value – beauty is down to the designer and the audience!

precious plastic jewellery: projects

pressure-laminated acrylic

INSPIRATION

Reptile skins and metallic beetles
Inspired by the texture of reptile scales and metallic beetles with carapaces that resemble exotic metal, the piece uses the texture and colour as the basis for the design.

DESIGN

The design is a simplified form of the beetle shape, maintaining the basic form but losing the details that make it recognisable as an insect. The design was chosen to ensure that the final piece is elegant, simple and wearable, rather than too flamboyant and dramatic, making it attractive to a wide audience while still being unusual and unique.

Step 1 – Materials: pressure-laminated acrylic and silver fitting

Step 2 – Acrylic cut to shape

Step 3 – Sanding acrylic to profile

Step 4 – Polished acrylic pieces

Step 5 – Finished fitting and acrylic elements

FITTINGS

The fitting is constructed from 0.9 mm sterling silver sheet; silver wire and a simple pendant bail is used to attach the fitting to a chain.

PLASTICS

The plastic used is two pieces of 5 mm clear extruded acrylic sheet. The two pieces are pressure-laminated together (see Pressure-laminating pages 82–84). The material between the two layers is fine metallic foil, cotton threads and iridescent film from Christmas decorations.

ASSEMBLY

The acrylic is pressed, marked out, cut and sanded to shape and then polished. The individual pieces are then carefully fitted into the fabricated silver fitting and fixed into place using superglue. The whole piece is then given a final polish.

FINISHED PIECE

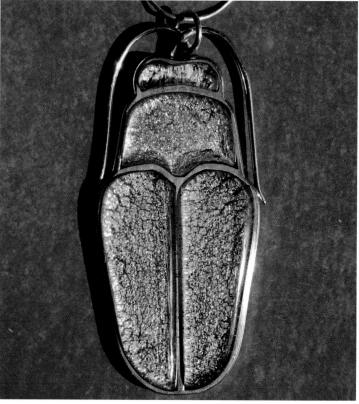

Step 6 – The finished piece

polypropylene flower jewellery

Step 1 – Dyeing polypropylene

Step 2 – Thermoforming polypropylene using acrylic as a heat shield

Step 3 – Selection of shaped polypropylene petals

INSPIRATION

Passion flower or star lily

The natural world can provide a wide range of inspiration: the star lilies grown by my father provided the inspiration for this piece. The large, elegant and colourful flowers, with their complex forms and details made interpreting them into a piece of jewellery a challenge.

DESIGN

The design uses the form and colours of the original flowers but breaks down some of the elements into individual pieces to create more depth in the final piece.

FITTINGS

The fitting is constructed from 0.7 mm sterling silver sheet and silver tube to produce a large, flamboyant piece.

PLASTICS

Polypropylene is used throughout this piece (with the exception of the central stamens, which are acrylic) and the individual elements dyed to give the required colours and textures. The polypropylene is also gently heated and distorted to create the texture of the petals, using acrylic as a heat shield.

ASSEMBLY

The polypropylene is dyed to give the required colours, using two disperse dyes, and then marked out and cut into the rough shapes of the petals; they are then heat-treated to add further texture.

    The individual elements are then trimmed and glued into the fabricated silver fitting and the piece is given a final clean and polish.

FINISHED PIECE

Step 4 – Silver fitting fabricated

Step 5 – Polypropylene petals glued onto fitting

Step 6 – The finished piece

examples of artists currently working with plastics

Perspex lace cuff bangle Laser cut, heat formed acrylic. 48 x 3.5 x 0.8 cm. Photograph by Rory Moore, Belfast.

Rachel McKnight

Rachel McKnight studied at the University of Ulster in Belfast. Since graduating in 2003, Rachel produces necklaces, bangles, earrings, rings and brooches to form quirky creations in plastics and rubber. The excitement of sourcing new materials and experimenting with them inspires her to produce original and innovative jewellery. The idea of transparency and opaque colour influences her designs, and plastics allow her to explore this. Simple, uncomplicated shapes and the concept of duplicating shapes also form the basis for Rachel's jewellery.

Not only does Rachel have a large range of small batch production, but she also likes the challenge of producing larger scale work for exhibitions and collections.

Originally, Rachel hand cut all of her work, but in the last couple of years she has embraced technology and now cuts most work using a laser cutter. The idea of combining a man-made, industrial product with a delicate and traditional pattern inspires her work.

These pieces were inspired by Tudor ruffs. Rachel loved their simplicity and the duplication of basic forms, and wanted to recreate a modern version made from polypropylene plastic using a laser cutter.

White twisted ruffle collar Laser cut polypropylene and nylon-coated stainless steel. Photograph by Trevor Hart, Dublin.

All images copyright of Rachel McKnight & individual photographers

Gill Forsbrook

My jewellery is made from plastics and metals; sheet plastics, especially polypropylene, being the predominant material.

Some of the qualities of plastics that interest me are colour, translucency, transparency and flexibility. I aim to exploit these qualities in my work.

The design of my work develops from an exploration of the materials that I choose to use.

I use basic metalwork and jewellery techniques. I cut, drill, score, fold and wrap the flexible sheet plastics.

I am interested in finding different ways to hold the plastics in position. For different pieces I find different solutions, sometimes fabricating fittings and fixings from metal or using threads such as braided nylon to knot or bind pieces together.

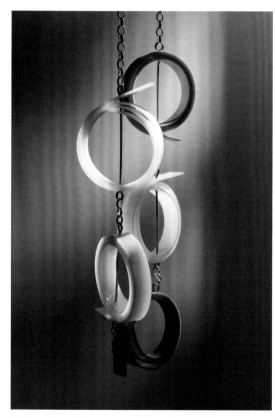

Chain necklace Polypropylene, silver. 48 x 3.5 x 0.8 cm

All images copyright of Gill Forsbrook

Large flexible bangle Polypropylene, polycarbonate, silver. 15 x 13 x 3 cm. The loops inside the bangle are flexible and the arm pushes through the central loop.

Choker Polypropylene, silver. 5.5 cm high x 36 cm long

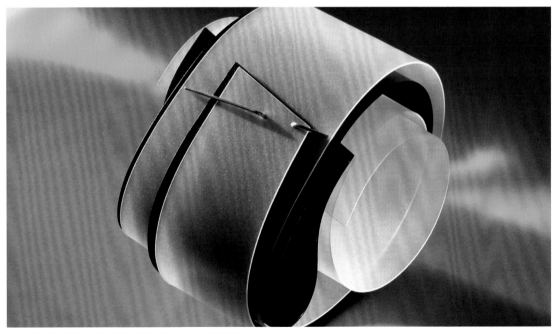

Large black, white and red bangle Polypropylene, PVC, silver. 10 x 12 x 9 cm

Tusheeta David

Through my work I aim to create jewellery that reflects my influences, inspiration and identity. Having grown up in a country with soaring levels of skill, developing traditional jewellery manufacturing skills did not excite me. The application of current technologies in contemporary crafts drew my attention and I resolved to use it as a tool to venture into uncharted territories.

The unglamorous ubiquity of plastics and their availability in a range of colours allured me to explore their properties further. Colour is crucial to my design aesthetic, and I combine hand-dyed bright colours with fluorescent acrylic. My work explores the play of light with acrylic by virtue of its properties of edge lighting and transparency.

I am inspired by the mystery that highly microscopic images exude; a sense of wonder of a parallel life veiled beneath perceived existence. I use these microscopic images from nature to create highly magnified digital patterns using CAD. I have used laser technology to push the boundaries of what was perceived to be possible. Thermoforming techniques assist me in creating simple yet clever forms in acrylic that act as the canvas for these elaborate patterns. The result is a magnificent symbiosis of colour, form, material and technology.

Sheets of acrylic are rescued from landfill and recycled to create jewellery that incorporates clever nuances and architecture to deliver a visual product that is stunning by virtue of its theatrical scale and form.

Jaundiced coral bracelet Thermoformed, laser cut hand-dyed acrylic. 18 x 16 x 5 cm

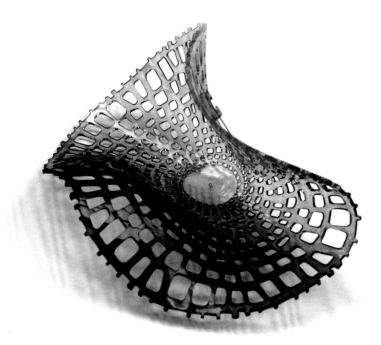

Cell brooch Thermoformed, laser cut hand-dyed acrylic and stainless steel. 19 x 14 x 9 cm

appendix 1:
constructing a vacuum-former

A basic vacuum-former can be constructed simply and cheaply from MDF (medium density fibreboard), a few strips of metal and a household vacuum cleaner.

The dimensions used in this example were based on the largest piece of plastic that would fit into a domestic oven (which is used to heat the plastic before forming). The same principle could be used on a smaller scale if the design is rescaled accordingly.

This vacuum-former consists of a double-chambered vacuum box and a metal frame to support the plastic sheet.

The vacuum box is constructed of the following materials (all panels cut from 13 mm MDF):
- 2 boards 400 x 400 mm
- 4 boards 387 x 100 mm
- 4 boards 387 x 35 mm.

Take one of the 400 mm-square boards and mark a line 40 mm from each edge, leaving a square that is 360 mm x 360 mm. Then mark lines at 20 mm intervals (19 marks) along each side. Draw lines across the board to form a grid. Drill 4.5 mm holes at each intersection and along the outline of the grid, creating a pattern of 361 holes.

Take the other 400 mm-square board and glue the four 387 x 100 mm boards onto one side to create an open-topped box. (Ensure that the boards touch and that all joints are sealed with wood glue.)

Take the drilled board and glue this onto the box as a lid.

Take the 387 x 35 mm boards and glue them onto the top of the drilled board, creating an open-topped box, again ensure that the edges are sealed with wood glue. This forms the basic vacuum box. On the top edge of the open box, glue a thick strip of soft leather, heat-resistant rubber or some other suitable material that will form a seal when the plastic is placed onto the box in the metal frame.

Drill a hole through the middle of one of the 387 x 100 mm boards, large enough to fit a vacuum cleaner pipe through – this should be a tight fit to ensure that a good vacuum is created inside the bottom chamber when the vacuum cleaner is switched on.

Make a 400 x 400 mm metal frame from approximately 16 x 2 mm flat steel strips – welded at the corners. Drill two holes along each edge, then take four strips of 16 x 2 x 365 mm and drill holes to match those in the frame. A plastic sheet can then be cut to form a 400 x 400 mm sheet and holes made to secure it into the frame. Insert eight bolts through the frame, plastic and securing strip and tighten to ensure that the plastic is secure.

The frame with the plastic can then be placed onto the seal on top of the vacuum-former – check that the seal is as airtight as possible.

The vacuum-former is then ready for use. For the best results, place the vacuum-former into an oven equipped with an internal grill element – allow 100–150 mm between the heating element and the plastic sheet, switch on the grill and wait until the plastic softens. When the plastic is sufficiently softened, switch on the vacuum and the plastic will be sucked down onto the drilled board and moulded over any item placed on the drilled board.

This process requires a degree of practice and testing to achieve the best results, as differences in oven performance, material thickness and type and distance from the element will all affect the time required to heat the plastic.

The finished vacuum-former

appendix 2:

health & safety and environmental information quick reference chart

Health & safety Polypropylene	Recycling Polypropylene	Biodegradability Polypropylene
Combustion releases carbon monoxide and carbon dioxide, which represent a hazard to health. For further details you should contact the supplier and request a Material Safety Data Sheet.	Plastics Recycling Symbol Number 5 – PP. Commonly recycled, however the main issue that impacts on the level of recycling is the recovery of the items after use. With increasing emphasis on recycling, it is likely that the percentage of polypropylene recovered each year will increase. ♺ 5 PP	Without the addition of UV-absorbing additives and anti-oxidants, polypropylene is susceptible to UV degradation which will result in the breakdown of the polymer and the appearance of surface cracks that become deeper over time as the degradation continues. In jewellery applications it is unlikely that the material will receive sufficient UV exposure to cause any notable damage.

Health & safety Acrylic, perspex or plexiglas	Recycling Acrylic, perspex or plexiglas	Biodegradability Acrylic, perspex or plexiglas
Combustion results in the release of carbon dioxide, water, methyl methacrylate and carbon monoxide. The quantity of carbon monoxide released will depend on the temperature and the amount of available oxygen, however this represents a toxic hazard and should be avoided. The polishing and sanding of acrylic can create dust. Although this does not represent a toxic hazard, it is possible that quantities of the dust may irritate the respiratory system and it is advisable to use a suitable dust mask and extraction, where possible.	Plastics Recycling Symbol Number 7 – Plastics Other. There is currently limited recycling of acrylic and this is usually in the form of industrial recycling where the material is re-ground and made into pellets for re-use. However, this is at a relatively low level and most acrylic ends up in landfill sites. This is mainly because of the relative difficulty of recycling acrylic. It is possible to de-polymerise the resin but the process involves hazardous materials that can contaminate the recovered material. However, new technology may improve this process in the future.	Most acrylic ends up in landfill sites where it only degrades at a slow rate.
Health & safety **Nylon**	**Recycling** **Nylon**	**Biodegradability** **Nylon**
With the variety of polymers that are covered under the generic name 'nylon', it is only possible to generalise about the risks. Specific research should be conducted on the grade of nylon used to determine what hazards may be associated with its use and disposal. Some nylons break down in fire, producing smoke, fumes or ash that may contain hydrogen cyanide. Hydrogen cyanide is highly toxic and can cause death in under 60 seconds at sufficient concentration, therefore it is essential that any nylon residue is disposed of with care and not incinerated.	Plastics Recycling Symbol Number 7 – Plastics Other. There is currently limited recycling of nylon and this is usually in the form of industrial recycling where the material is re-ground and palletised for re-use. However, this is at a relatively low level and most nylon ends up in landfill sites. This is mainly because of the wide variety of nylon polymers and the range of colours that are produced, making it difficult to separate and recycle in economic quantities. **7** **Other**	Only degrades at a slow rate.

Health & safety — Polystyrene

High-temperature incineration of polystyrene produces mainly carbon dioxide, water and soot with some volatile compounds. However, at lower temperatures it will produce carbon monoxide, styrene monomers and other polycyclic aromatic hydrocarbons which are known as carcinogenic, mutagenic, and teratogenic. Therefore it is not recommended that polystyrene should be disposed of by burning in a domestic environment

Recycling — Polystyrene

Plastics Recycling Symbol Number 6.
Due to its low value and the problems of recycling foamed forms, it is not commonly recycled and is not generally collected at roadside recycling points. However, industrial recycling is increasing.the amount of material recovered. New technology may improve this process in the future.

6 PS

Biodegradability — Polystyrene

Not biodegradable (lifetime estimated as 500 years or more). This means that the majority of polystyrene waste will form landfill, where it will remain almost indefinitely. Added to this is the impact of foamed polystyrene which forms a serious pollutant in aquatic environments, where it floats on the surface and can travel vast distances.

Health & safety — Polyethylene

The combustion of polyethylene produces carbon dioxide, carbon monoxide and aldehydes as well as other by-products, dependant on the type of polyethylene. Therefore it is not advisable to burn residual material, and areas contaminated by smoke etc. should be ventilated thoroughly.

Recycling — Polyethylene

LDPE – Plastics Recycling Symbol Number 4.
HDPE – Plastics Recycling Symbol Number 2.
Recyclable, but significant quantities find their way into landfill where they will not degrade quickly.

4 LDPE

2 HDPE

Biodegradability — Polyethylene

UV exposure does degrade polyethylene and there have been suggestions that bacteria may be effective at degrading polyethylene in a relatively short period of time, given the right environmental conditions. However, this is not currently common practice.

Health & safety PVC or polyvinyl chloride	Recycling PVC or polyvinyl chloride	Biodegradability PVC or polyvinyl chloride
On combustion, PVC can release hydrogen chloride which will dissolve in water to produce hydrochloric acid. In addition to this, the combustion of PVC releases dioxins (polychlorinated dibenzodioxins and dibenzofurans), these materials are known to bioaccumulate, are mutagenic and carcinogenic, and are therefore considered to be serious environmental pollutants and a risk to health. Plasticisers used in the modification of PVC polymer, particularly diethylhexyl phthalate, have been cited as a possible hazard to human health, however the level of exposure in jewellery applications is probably insignificant. The use of PVC cement in bonding releases solvents into the area adjacent to the material. Care should be taken to ensure sufficient ventilation. It is essential that the manufacturer's instructions and safety information are read and understood before using PVC cement.	Plastics Recycling Symbol Number 3. Due to the low cost of producing PVC and the relatively high cost of collection and reprocessing, the recycling of PVC has been relatively low. However, legislation and new recycling methods are leading to a gradual increase in the recovery of PVC materials. 3 V	PVC is not biodegradable, and remains in the environment. In addition to this problem, it has been suggested that PVC may leach chemicals into the groundwater, causing contamination and posing a health risk. Therefore the re-use or recycling of PVC should be encouraged.

suppliers

The main manufacturers are extremely reluctant to deal with individuals and will not supply sheets in small quantities. Therefore the best source of material is currently from a third-party distributor – usually a paper merchant, plastics distributor or processor.

Few of these third parties will carry the full range of colours at any one time. They will tend to focus on the higher volume colours or new variations, and as a result it may be difficult to obtain some of the colours in a manufacturer's colour swatch.

In order to ensure that the maximum range of colours is available, it is important to contact as many potential suppliers as possible and to request the following information:

▶ minimum order quantity
▶ carriage charge
▶ colour range available
▶ thicknesses available
▶ price per sheet (standard sheet sizes are 650 x 1100 mm).

Some suppliers may be willing to supply material through their samples service, which allows for small orders to be processed.

As with most materials, the cost will vary considerably from different sources and depending on the quantities that are ordered. The rising cost of raw materials, particularly oil prices, tends to be reflected in a rise in the price of plastics.

The websites listed below are constantly being updated and additional products listed, and so it is recommended that anyone searching for materials consults a wide range of suppliers, even if they are listed under different material headings.

general UK suppliers

http://www.plasticstockist.com
http://www.shopforplastic.co.uk/smaller-quantities-95-c.asp
http://www.righton.co.uk/products.cfm
http://www.bayplastics.co.uk/index.htm

polypropylene sheet

http://www.priplak.com (France – manufacturer)
http://www.roberthorne.co.uk/products/brand/priplak (UK)
http://www.hobarts.com/store (UK)
http://www.plaspro.co.uk (UK)
http://www.cppltd.com/Sheet-Materials/index.html (UK)
http://www.corbiplastics.com/products/solid-plastic-sheets.htm (USA)
http://www.westwardplastics.co.uk/schools.php (UK)
http://www.rapidonline.com/Education/Graphics/Plastics (UK)
http://www.conservation-by-design.co.uk
http://www.plastim.co.uk – Limited range of colours available but
   willing to supply ten sheets at time
http://www.atlasplastics.co.uk
http://www.folia.de

NB
The suppliers listed below advertise these materials for sale online or direct. However, availability, order quantities and costs cannot be guaranteed and it is recommended that designers conduct a thorough search for materials locally before ordering.

acrylic

http://www.roberthornedirect.co.uk (UK)
http://www.atlasplastics.co.uk/distribution.htm (UK)
http://www.hobarts.com/store (UK)
http://www.provincialrubber.co.uk/engineering-plastics/display-plastics.html (UK)
http://www.westwardplastics.co.uk/schools.php (UK)
http://www.gcip.co.uk/EP/perspex_sheet.htm (UK)
http://www.plastic stockist.com (UK)

mirrored acrylic

http:/www.roberthornedirect.co.uk (UK)
http://www.gcip.co.uk/EP/perspex_sheet.htm (UK)
http://www.plasticstockist.com (UK)

Acrylic is available in a wide range of forms including:
- cast acrylic sheet (3–150 mm)
- extruded acrylic sheet (1.5–10 mm)
- round rod (5–200 mm)
- square rod (3–75 mm)
- triangular rod (4–25 mm)
- half-round rod (10–25 mm)
- tube (5–650 mm).

PRICES
Acrylic varies in price depending on the size and thickness of the material and the quantity purchased. However, as acrylic is a material that is readily available and is used in many applications, it may be possible to obtain offcuts at very reasonable prices or even free, in small quantities, from a manufacturer processing acrylic sheet.

nylon

http://www.gcip.co.uk/EP/materials/nylon_ertalon_rod_sheet_tube.htm (UK)
http://www.provincialrubber.co.uk/engineering-plastics/engineering-plastics.html (UK)
http://www.westwardplastics.co.uk/schools.php (UK)

polystyrene

Sheet polystyrene seems to be more readily available than some other plastics, probably due to its use within the model-making industry.

However, due to the nature of the material the available thicknesses of the sheets tends to range from 1 mm upwards. A standard range of thicknesses is probably 1, 2 and 3 mm, though some manufacturers may produce materials to other specifications.

A range of colours can be obtained including the following:

- white
- black
- clear
- red
- mid blue
- dark blue
- green
- yellow
- silver
- ivory
- orange
- purple
- opal
- gold – mirror
- silver – mirror

Stockists include: www.educationalsupplies.co.uk (search for polystyrene)

POLYSTYRENE SHEET

Sheets available as 1 mm sheets of 508 x 458 mm (red, orange, yellow, green, blue, black, white, brown, gold and silver).
http://www.plasticstockist.com (UK)
http://www.esheet.co.uk (UK)
http://www.roberthornedirect.co.uk (UK)

PVC

PVC SHEET

http://www.educationalsupplies.co.uk (UK)

Sheets available as 0.7 mm clear sheets of 610 x 458 mm.
www.specialistcrafts.co.uk (UK)

0.4 mm clear sheets of 508 x 458 mm
0.14 mm clear sheets of 450 x 635 mm
http://www.roberthornedirect.co.uk (UK)
http://www.westwardplastics.co.uk/schools.php (UK)
http://www.pvcsheet.co.uk/ (UK)
http://www.folia.de

polyethylene

http://www.westwardplastics.co.uk/schools.php (UK)
http://www.bayplastics.co.uk/polyethylene (UK)
http://www.directplasticsonline.co.uk (UK)

dyes

http://www.kemtex.co.uk (UK)
http://www.prochemicalanddye.com/home.php (US)
http://www.avocet-dyes.co.uk (UK)
http://www.pburch.net/dyeing/acrylic.shtml#dyewithdisperse (US)

adhesives

CYANOACYLATES SUPPLIERS

K+S Industriebedarf GmbH
    Steige 4 – D-69436 Schwanheim, Tel: 0049 62 62 38 99
    www.ks-klebstoffe.de
    For technical support contact: info@ks-klebstoffe.de

Green Hobby and Model, the R/C source
38 Clareville Road, Harolds Cross, Dublin 6W, Tel: 00353 1 4928776
http://www.greenhobbymodel.com/glues.html
    For sales, contact: norman@greenhobbymodel.com

http://www.bondrite.co.uk/cyanoacylates/cat_2.html (UK)
http://www.gluguru.com/Ciba2000.htm (US)
http://www.screwfix.com (UK) (search for polyurethane adhesive)
http://www.holdich.demon.co.uk/chemical/balcotan/100.htm (UK)
http://www.geedee-modelshop.com/prodlist.asp?SubCategoryID=230&offset=40 (UK)
http://www.mcguckin.com (US) (search for 'cyano')

PLASTIC WELD SUPPLIERS

EMA Plastic Weld (liquid solvent cement)
    EMA Model Supplies Limited
    Unit 2, Shepperton Business Park
    Govett Avenue
    Shepperton
    TW17 8BA
    Tel: 01932 228228
    FAX: 01932 253766
http://www.ema-models.co.uk (UK)

laser cutter manufacturers

http://www.cut-tec.co.uk (UK)

routers & milling machines

http://www.visionengravers.com (US)

vacuum-formers

http://www.technologysupplies.co.uk (UK)
http://www.crclarke.co.uk/Products/VF/VF.html (UK)
http://www.widgetworksunlimited.com/Vacuum_Formers_s/35.htm (US)

suppliers of plastics outside the UK

USA

http://www.calsakplastics.com
http://www.onlinemetalsupply.com
http://www.delviesplastics.com
http://www.interstateplastics.com
http://www.eplastics.com
http://www.professionalplastics.com

AUSTRALIA

http://pearlplastiks.com.au
http://www.acrylicsonline.com.au
http://www.modularplastics.com.au
http://ausplastics.com.au
http://www.acrilixplastics.com.au

useful websites

Robert Horne Group – suppliers of a wide range of plastics etc.
http://www.roberthorne.co.uk/products/results/Plastics

Properties of polymers website:
http://www.polymerprocessing.com/polymers/index.html
http://www.plasticsindustry.org

For an acrylic handbook
http://www.atlasplastics.co.uk/acrylic.htm

glossary

Basic dye – a type of dye used for dyeing paper, silk, wood and acrylic.

Channel fittings – a fitting with a U-shaped cross section into which plastic elements can be secured using a suitable adhesive. The fitting secures the elements in place and provides an aesthetically appealing finish.

Differential dyeing – dyeing a piece of material more than one colour by placing part of the material in a dye bath of one colour and, once this portion has been dyed, placing another part of the material in a dye bath of a different colour.

Disperse dye – a type of dye used for dyeing polyester and acetate etc. The dye molecules are the smallest of all dyes.

Disperse dyeing – the process of dyeing a material using a disperse dye.

Dye bath – a durable, usually metal or ceramic, container used to hold the dye solution while dyeing an object. Dye baths are frequently fitted with a heating element and may be sealed to increase pressure and temperature.

Gel phase – the state between a hard solid and a fully melted plastic. The body of the plastic becomes flexible and mouldable and the surface becomes 'tacky'. It will then bond to other pieces of the same plastic by heat fusion.

Heat fusion – the bonding of plastic by heating two or more pieces until the polymer softens sufficiently to allow them to bond when pressed together.

Hot-foil blocking – a common commercial print process where metallic foil is applied to a material by stamping a heated die onto the foil and then onto the material, adhering it to the surface and leaving the design of the die on the material.

Linisher – a belt sanding machine used to grind a surface to improve its flatness and smoothness.

Micro-cracking – microscopic cracks that form in the structure of the plastic when the polymer is overstressed. They appear as a milky discolouration in the plastic and cannot be removed. The discolouration is caused by the refraction of light through the cracks.

Micron (or micrometre) – this is by definition 1×10^{6} of a metre i.e. one millionth of a metre (or one thousandth of a millimetre) 0.001 mm.

Plastic memory – the ability of a plastic polymer to recover its previous form when exposed to heat. The heat must be sufficient to allow the polymer to relax any stresses caused post-thermoforming but not so much as to allow the polymer to melt. For example, if a strip of polypropylene is curled up and left in a box for a period of time, when removed it will remain partially curled. By applying a gentle heat the strip will uncurl.

Power file – a commercial power tool similar to a belt sander or linisher, but smaller and hand-held rather than bench-mounted. It is used to grind material into shape.

Pressure laminating – the bonding of layers of plastic, particularly acrylic, by heat fusion and the application of pressure. Other materials can be encapsulated between the layers of plastic to produce aesthetically pleasing results.

Slide plate – a fitting that consists of two plates, one with a keyhole-shaped slot or slots, and the other with a projection that passes through the larger opening of the keyhole and slides down to the narrow part of the slot, thereby securing the two plates together.

Swarf – the debris or waste resulting from cutting, milling or grinding of a material.

Thermoforming – the process of forming or moulding a material that is softened using heat. The new shape is permanent once cooled, unless reheated.

Thermoplastic – a plastic that can be moulded, cast or formed when heated to a liquid or semi-liquid state.

Thermoset – a plastic that has been formed into shape while hot and, when cooled, is permanently set. The repeated application of heat after setting does not allow these plastics to be remoulded.

Ultrasonic welding – an industrial technique whereby high-frequency ultrasonic acoustic vibrations are applied locally to materials that are being held together under pressure to create a solid-state weld.

index